CW01509007

YOUR SECRET POWER

HOW TO NOURISH YOUR BODY, MIND & SOUL FOR SELF-MASTERY & MIRACLES

DEBBIE STURGE

To Mags
with love
Debbie 💗

authors
AND CO.

Copyright © 2020 by Debbie Sturge

ISBN: 978-1-913728-04-5

All rights reserved.
No part of this book may be reproduced in any form or by any electronic or
mechanical means, including information storage and retrieval systems,
without written permission from the author, except for the use of brief
quotations in a book review.

DEDICATION

To Paul, my husband, best friend, rock and guru all rolled into one. Thank you for always being there and for your love, encouragement, support & belief in me.

In memory of my dear Dad, my absolute hero.

CONTENTS

ACKNOWLEDGEMENTS

I am so deeply grateful to all the amazing people in my life who have helped bring this book to fruition, either directly or indirectly, to turn a childhood dream into a reality. I have been blessed with so many teachers; those who have inspired and motivated me and those who played a pivotal role in ensuring I faced important life lessons. Each and every one of you has shaped me into the person I am today.

A massive thank you to my family, for tolerating my highs and lows over the years and for not giving up on me. For my husband Paul in particular for his sense of humour, positive attitude and common sense approach to life that's kept me grounded on many an occasion... and sane! Paul, I love you with all my heart, and while I'm sure there must have been times you wondered about my choices, I thank you for respecting them regardless and for never doubting me, even when I did myself. You have always been my rock and biggest supporter, and if it wasn't for you, this book would definitely not have been written.

Heartfelt thanks to my best friends Fi Duncan and Vicky Waters for your unwavering support, especially when I needed it most; I love you guys! And to all my wonderful friends who have cheered me on over the years, helped me grow and realise my potential. Also, Tina Pavlou and my beautiful Reiki sisters at The Goddess Rooms, who lifted me up when my heart's wings forgot how to fly. And, of course, the Universe for having faith in me that there was nothing I couldn't handle and for always having my back.

I'd also like to acknowledge loved ones lost, especially my dear dad and younger brother David. Dad, you always believed in me and knew I had a book in me, and Dave, I was so proud of you and all you had accomplished. I hope you're both proud of me now and are looking down, smiling. I love you, and miss you.

Special thanks to Abigail Horne for all the amazing training, tips and support within the Author's Academy, for your belief in me that I had a book to share and for instigating the process. And thank you to Lucy Crane, Authors & Co and all the other powerful, inspirational women in the Author's Academy who helped to keep me going. Sincere thanks also to Yasmin Yarwood of Meticulous Proofreading and to my other beta readers Fi Duncan, Joanne Powell and Rebecca Nicks. Your feedback, comments and support were invaluable.

Thanks also to my many clients over the years and everyone who has followed me, interacted on Facebook and took the time to watch my videos. Hearing how much I'd helped and inspired you was significant in my realisation of the value I had to offer and encouraged me to put pen to paper.

And last but by no means least, I'd like to thank YOU, my reader. Whatever synchronistic events may have led you to pick up this book and bring us together, it is my sincerest desire that our onward journey inspires you to shine your light and fulfil your higher purpose. Thank you for granting me this opportunity to help you step into your secret power.

I love you all.

Debbie xx

INTRODUCTION

MY SPIRITUAL AWAKENING

I haven't always been interested in personal growth, expanding my consciousness or spirituality, but mostly because I knew so little, if anything about it. Neither was I naturally a positive, upbeat person. My default setting was as a glass half empty kind of a girl. I anticipated worse case scenarios, expected people to let me down and blamed everyone else when something went wrong.

Over the years I've battled with self-doubt, limiting beliefs, fear of failure (and success), and for a long time I felt like I was treading water, unclear of my direction in life and what I 'should' be doing. In my gut, I believed I was destined to fulfil a larger purpose, but just what it was, I had absolutely no idea. I knew I wanted to help others, empathy has always been one of my strengths, and I genuinely care about people, but it took me many years to realise I needed to work on myself first.

However, with this knowledge came the opportunity for change. For every challenge I encountered, and at every crossroad I reached, I was presented with an opportunity to learn and grow, or to shrink back in fear. In the early days, it was very much the latter, but the more I worked on my mindset, personal development and spiritual growth, the more I noticed positive steps going forward. And with this growth came newfound confidence to keep going, to continue the work and my journey. I was no longer afraid to leave the safety of my comfort zone, and I felt ready to step into my power.

Over the years, my journey has taken many twists and turns. Among the good times, there have been others where I've felt stretched and tested to the max. I lost my dad to cancer while learning to cope with my mum's dementia and then only fourteen months later, my younger brother was killed in an accident. More recently, my husband has had his own battle with cancer, and we faced our biggest challenge to date. But one thing I'm sure of now is that it's often these most difficult challenges that become our greatest learning experiences. We just have to have faith.

If anything the struggles I've faced have made me more passionate to help others. But not just to cope with challenges, my ultimate aim is to inspire you to follow your dreams, to believe anything is possible with the right mindset and action, and to help you become the best version of yourself. It's what I strive for, and what you deserve. But first and to help provide a level of perspective, I'd like to share a little more about my own journey.

I grew up with my parents and two brothers in a quiet seaside town, relatively happy and carefree. It was a strict upbringing, and mum was a force to be reckoned with, but dad was a big softy and my absolute hero. I was introduced to organised religion very early on as mum was quite heavily involved with the church, but while I enjoyed listening to bible stories in Sunday school as a young child, I soon began to question it all. By my teens, I had decided it was irritatingly uncool and not for me. I was having a hard enough time finding my way, without believing 'God' would answer my prayers.

I very rarely took a stand against mum, but the time came when I refused to go to church. Organised religion was far too pompous, stuffy and outdated in my opinion, and I was also fed up with the hypocrisy I witnessed among some of the regular churchgoers. As far as I was concerned, it didn't make me a bad person not making the weekly pilgrimage to church, any more than it made anyone else a good person simply for going. And if there was such a thing as God, I felt absolutely sure he'd agree.

While I've always believed in there being a higher power, it was the whole concept of God that I struggled with for many years due to the association with organised religion. Even now I prefer to use terms like the Universe, Spirit, Source Energy, or the Creator of all that is rather than

God, although I am well aware now they are one of the same.

By contrast to my happy childhood, my teenage years were troubled and rebellious, and at times I was intensely unhappy. I never seemed to fit in despite being desperate to do so, and I was bullied at school for no end of reasons. I studied hard because I wanted my parents to be proud of me, but the good grades I achieved, as a result, meant I was highly unpopular with my peers. I just couldn't win. In an attempt to toughen up, I adopted a 'don't care' attitude and started to skip school. By the time I reached my final year, I was also smoking, drinking and sleeping around. I knew it wasn't me, but the bullying had left its mark.

Unfortunately, these scars went on to set the stage for far too many years of my adult life. Low confidence, self-esteem and self-worth, fear of speaking up, of being judged and ridiculed, the need to always seek approval, people-pleasing, you name it; I've struggled with all of this emotional baggage! Although deep inside, I knew I wanted to make something of my life, I was scared to shine my light for fear of attracting the bullying all over again.

Rather than staying on at school and continuing my education which was very much my parents' wishes, I left at the earliest available opportunity, took the first job I could get and stepped into uncertain independence. Not that it lasted long. I met my husband that same summer, was engaged on my seventeenth birthday and married two and a half years later.

Despite being blessed with two amazing children in my early 20's, I suffered postnatal depression and hit an all-time low. I felt like a failure as a mother and as a wife. It's like I woke up one day and couldn't remember who I was. I'd completely lost my own identity and self-worth. But while a part of me believed that my husband and children would be better off without me, I couldn't shrug an inner feeling that there had to be more to life. I knew I owed it to myself, and my family to find out what it was.

I now know this was when my spiritual journey really began. I started reading about angels and came across Louise Hay's book 'You Can Heal Your Life'. I was also led to 'The Celestine Prophecy' by James Redfield, which I found fascinating. Desperate to find my purpose, this all but confirmed my gut feeling that the Universe does have a plan for us all. We each have a predetermined mission to complete. I was finally waking up and began to feel more hopeful that things were not as dark as I'd previously thought. I just needed to find my way.

My newfound faith led me towards complementary therapies and a brand new career. In September 1999, after an intense three-year training, I graduated with distinction to become a nutritional therapist. I felt immensely proud of my achievement and was sure I'd found my calling. How could it get any better? I was finally able to help people and make a real difference, and it was incredibly rewarding. And I'm not going to lie; it did wonders to rebuild my previously shattered self-esteem. But as time went on, I realised it was not unfolding as I'd hoped and once again I felt as though something was missing.

It was early days on my spiritual path, and I was still very closed-minded. One of the reasons nutritional therapy had appealed to me was because it was science-backed and, in my opinion, very black and white. I believed everyone could be cured by simply changing their diet, taking some tailored nutritional supplements and incorporating exercise into their daily regime. Frustratingly, the reality didn't turn out to be quite so straightforward.

I noticed how some people would sabotage their own efforts towards change, or have such a negative mindset and low self-worth that they simply didn't have the belief they could achieve the results they wanted. And so they didn't, regardless of whether or not they changed their diet. By contrast, I had some clients come to me with health issues, despite the fact they were already following a fabulously healthy diet. These clients posed challenges of a different kind. While diagnostic testing may have revealed a more complex underlying issue, there was often no logical explanation as to why they weren't getting the results I'd have expected them to. Were they all simply getting in their own way, or was I missing something?

Without a doubt, nutrition is a powerful healer, and I am a passionate advocate for it. I have been able to help many clients over the years. However, over the course of these years and noticing some of the discrepancies I've mentioned, I was naturally led to a far more open-minded approach to health. And I began to realise that in order to achieve optimal health and wellbeing, we simply couldn't ignore the mind, body and spirit connection.

I developed a strong fascination with the power of the mind, while my interest in more spiritual healing disciplines also grew. By now, I was regularly meditating and incorporating other techniques you'll find outlined in this book, and I was led to learn Reiki, an ancient Japanese energy healing modality. For something that would have been far too woo woo for me only a few years earlier, it soon became very close to my heart, and I was able to offer it to my dad in his final months battling cancer, with very obvious results.

I've come to learn that personal and spiritual development is an ongoing process. You have to commit to working on yourself every day and understand that even if you already have dreams and set goals, they are likely to change over time. You must remain flexible and open to this, and if you can, there will be times you'll find surprising things happen. Sometimes, the very things you were once so desperate to achieve will pale to insignificance, as other new and exciting opportunities direct you along a different path.

There were numerous times in my life that I felt like a failure, but this was because my mindset was all wrong, and I was too rigid with my goals. Once I'd made up my mind about something I'd be like a dog with a bone, working relentlessly to almost try and force it to happen. But because I expected it to manifest in a very specific way and was totally blinkered to the possibility of something else, I would actually block it from happening. And to make matters worse, I'd often end up feeling totally overwhelmed and burnt out. Letting go of the outcome is something I've had to learn the hard way.

At the end of the day, it's not for us to know exactly how our dreams and goals will manifest. Quite often if things don't go to plan, it's because the Universe is conspiring to bring us something better. You may find it difficult to comprehend at the time and feel like a failure as I did, but further down the line, you may look back with relief that life took a different path. Take a moment to think about this now. Can you remember a time in your life when you were so disappointed not to have achieved a certain outcome, but can now look back and see it was for the best?

Another thing I've learned is how important it is to focus on the positives in life. Rather than beat yourself up for what you've not yet achieved, instead think about all the amazing things you have to date. I challenge you to make a note of them now. All of them! This has made a huge difference to me. Instead of focusing on any shortcomings, or things I may previously have thought I failed at, I now flip it around to hone in on all the pretty awesome things I have achieved, like reaching my black belt (2nd Dan) in karate in my late 40's!

My life is still very much a work in progress, but I'm no longer scared to follow my dreams, and I love the fact that this inspires others to take steps towards their own goals. Since fully embracing my spiritual path, I have become a traditional Usui, and Angelic Reiki Master/Teacher, a ThetaHealing® practitioner, a certified Spiritual/Transformation Life Coach, and I've studied EFT. I have also been drawn to various teaching and mentoring roles over the years.

Another massive dream of mine was realised in 2019 when I contributed to a powerful book collaboration and became co-author of 'When the Goddess Calls, Volume 2', which hit the Amazon bestseller list within a few hours of its release. A collection of powerful stories from women awakening on their spiritual path, I was honoured to feature alongside twelve other amazing and inspirational women.

True growth happens once we're brave enough to leave our comfort zone. It isn't always easy, and we have to get comfortable with being uncomfortable. Like peeling layers off an onion, we may celebrate a breakthrough one day, only to uncover something deeper, resulting in an emotional or spiritual detox the next. But believe me when I say, every moment will be worth it.

My intention for this book is to help you release any fear, self-sabotage, or belief that you are not good enough and by so doing, help you find your own path to greatness. I urge you to pay close attention to any resistance you may feel towards any part of this book, as it may be highlighting the very thing that's keeping you stuck and preventing you from moving forward. Ultimately I want you to understand some of the most important principles not only for holistic health but for self-mastery and miracles. I hope it inspires you to create the changes necessary to nourish your body, mind and soul, and to enable you to really step into and fully embrace YOUR SECRET POWER.

Let us begin...

PART 1 - ACKNOWLEDGE & ACCEPT

OUR FEAR-BASED EGO

Up until now, you may have imagined the path to spiritual awakening was one joyous journey involving endless retreats in exotic places, yoga on the beach at sunrise and meditating for hours in the lotus position with the smell of incense wafting on the breeze. If only! While you may, of course, be lucky to have this form part of your experience, the reality is likely to be very different. As I've said, it's often at our most challenging and desperate times that we set the foundations for our greatest spiritual and evolutionary leaps forwards. But we must be willing to have faith, to trust that the Universe always conspires to helps us and to surrender to the process. Which, of course, isn't always easy, or comfortable.

True spiritual awakening can only occur once we realise and accept that we are not our thoughts, emotions or beliefs, or the attachments we place upon them. This is our ego. Our true spiritual or higher self is the source of uncon-ditional love and is at one with the Universe. There is no separation and no 'self'. Our perception of self as an isolated, physical person is entirely the work of our ego.

Ego and awareness cannot coexist together. The ego strives to keep you separate from the world and operates from a position of fear, judgement and victimhood. Resistance, frustration, doubt, shame, struggle, sadness, feeling stuck, blaming or continually making excuses, are all indications your ego is getting the better of you. Ego is needy and loves drama. And it believes that in order for you to be complete and happy, you have to look outside of yourself. This may mean a new job, car, home or relationship, but something separate from you.

To be fair, our ego isn't all bad. In fact, we must give it credit where it's due, as without this foundation in fear the human race would not have survived. It has its purpose and works hard to keep us safe and protected. After all, if we were too chilled, we would not take threats seriously. But like an overbearing mother, it's constantly trying to thwart our growth, afraid of the unknown, or of us moving beyond our comfort zone. It likes to micromanage our every experience, to be in control. It is the voice of doubt in our ear, telling us we're not good enough, that it's not safe, or that we'll be ridiculed or criticised for trying something new. And it is always concerned with what others may think of us.

Looking back, I can see how hopelessly I played into the hands of my ego when my husband got sick and was subsequently diagnosed with cancer. I was totally gripped with fear in the early days and weeks. I experienced the fear of losing him, of being left alone and not able to cope, fear of not being strong enough for him or my family, and I was even fearful of his treatment and how he would respond to it. Unfortunately, once I was overwhelmed with fear, a whole host of other emotions took hold like resentment, grief, sadness and even anger. I was angry at the Universe as I believed I was either being tested on a monumental scale, or punished for reasons beyond my comprehension. I even felt angry at my husband for getting ill in the first place! And then I felt guilty about that... I was suffocating in victim mentality, blaming and judging, and then beating myself up.

I also felt very alone.

I knew I had no control whatsoever over the eventual outcome and couldn't bear it (ego). I became obsessed with reading everything cancer related, listening to podcasts and watching YouTube videos. I researched incessantly. I stopped working or doing any of my usual day-to-day activities to focus entirely on my husband and his recovery. I was absolutely desperate to 'save' him, or at least to do everything within my power with the tools and knowledge I was so fortunate to have, thanks to a background in nutritional therapy and Reiki. But I was making a huge mistake. I was trying to go it alone.

A Course in Miracles teaches us that the presence of fear is a sure sign we are trusting in our own strength, instead of tapping into the higher power of the Universe. I was so resistant and so fearful of the situation, with an ego so desperate to maintain some level of control, that I was actually well and truly stuck in the darkness. And it was incredibly dark for a while. I wanted to shut the whole world out until I figured a way through.

Fortunately, by using many of the tools and techniques within this book, I found my way back towards the light. I realised I had lost sight of the support and guidance available to each and every one of us and had become disconnected from Source. In order to reclaim my power, I knew I had to move away from fear and realign with love. Easier said than done you may think, and I'm not going to lie, but I took it step-by-step and paid a lot more attention to self-care, to meditation, prayer and Reiki.

As I was emerging from the darkness, I came across Matt Khan's book 'Everything is Here to Help You', and it massively resonated with me. I cannot recommend it enough. It made me realise I'd been way too hard on myself. The very thing I'd needed to do, surrender, is what tortures the ego the most and was the reason I'd found it so difficult. It's our ego that views the Universe on a reward versus punishment basis, but this simply isn't the case. The Universe does not punish us. It only ever wants the best for us. I knew this in my heart, but like many when faced with a particularly painful challenge, it was difficult to take on board in the midst of the chaos.

Khan writes that it's at these very challenging times that letting go of the outcome and admitting we don't know is the ultimate release. It signifies we are ready to walk the deeper path of our spiritual evolution. The ego is terrified of the unknown, and so it works hard to hold us back and keep us stuck. By contrast, even during periods of great loss and pain, the soul views this as an opportunity to make way for new experiences and to serve our highest expansion. Provided we dare to open up, this will set us on a more profound journey for the benefit of all.

Even at those times, you may find yourself in the depths of despair, as I did, it is crucial to understand there is always a deeper reason why this has happened. Each moment of pain indicates an energetic and emotional clearing that will ultimately allow you to fulfil the mission you've been incarnated to complete.

One very important thing to bear in mind is that any attempt on your part to move beyond pain or fear, to rid yourself of limiting beliefs or step outside your comfort zone will have the ego shift to panic mode faster than you can say DEFCON 1! This, in turn, can result in a spiritual detox of staggering proportions, where it may seem as if the Universe is massively conspiring against you. But understand this. As hard as it may seem if chaos surrounds you and everything seems to be going wrong, this is merely the work of the ego. It will do everything in its power to sabotage your efforts for growth and prevent you from venturing out into the unknown.

Regardless of our best intentions, we are often guilty of trying to control our circumstances and think we must take charge of a situation. This couldn't be further from the truth. Instead, we must have faith, express gratitude and allow the Universe to deliver. Your faith must be greater than your fear.

> "When you are grateful, fear disappears, and abundance appears."
>
> — TONY ROBBINS.

AWARE: Are you aware of your ego trying to control too much of your life? Do you struggle with emotions of fear, frustration or sadness, or find yourself blaming others for things that have happened to you? Are you scared to venture outside of your comfort zone, fearful of what might happen or what others may say? Can you see how this may be contributing to keeping you stuck? Are you currently relying too much on your own strength, instead of tapping into the power of the Universe?

ADJUST: Are there any adjustments you can make right now to give yourself a break? Even if only to take a deep breath and acknowledge where you're at and how you've been doing your best. Can you appreciate how far you've come and that by reading this book you've taken responsibility and a positive step forward?

ATTRACT: Your true, higher self is the part of you that operates directly according to your connection to Source energy; it is love-based and at one with the Universe. Trust your journey and allow good things to come to you. Whatever challenges you're facing right now, understand that everything is working out in perfect and divine timing. And you are never alone.

SOCIAL CONDITIONING & LIMITING BELIEFS

You'll find that throughout this book, I refer to the importance of raising your vibration and staying high vibe, but if this means nothing to you yet, please bear with me. I'll explain its significance in more detail throughout our journey, but suffice to say it's a crucial element in enabling your transition from fear and self-sabotage, to really stepping into your secret power towards self-mastery and miracles.

Even if you're unfamiliar with the concept of us being vibrational beings and know nothing about quantum physics, I'm sure it won't come as any surprise if I tell you that everything within our Universe is made up of energy. Each and every one of us is a unique energetic being, and we live in a vibrational universe where everything is connected. Everything is energy. And it follows that if you live in a state of high vibration you'll not only feel great, but you'll be able to manifest your every desire too. But more on this later…

For now, I want to focus on mindset because a positive or negative outlook along with what you tell yourself on a daily basis, will have a massive bearing on your vibration. But it's not simply a case of positive thinking which is probably just as well because let's face it; no one can be expected to have a positive mindset all the time! Even the most spiritual people among us will have their off days; we are human after all.

If we take into account how our mind works, it's easy to understand why. Our subconscious mind accounts for about 95% of how we see the world, while our conscious thoughts make up the remaining 5%, so tiny in comparison. Positive thinking is all well and good, and it definitely has its place, but it's the underlying chatter in our head that we really need to get a handle on!

Understanding and appreciating just how powerful your thoughts are is so important, as they can and will affect what shows up in your reality. Think of your mind as being like the control centre of your body, working tirelessly to create the life it perceives as being perfect for you. And this is the clue; it's all a matter of perception. If you carry self-limiting beliefs or negative thought patterns, it will be extremely difficult for you, if not impossible, to live the life you desire. So how do these beliefs come about in the first place?

When we are born, we are like a blank canvas of pure innocence and bliss. We love every wrinkle and crinkle of our body, have no fear of trying new things, nor do we have any doubt that all our needs will be met. It wouldn't cross our mind that we are anything other than perfect and we certainly wouldn't be worried about being too fat, too small, not intelligent enough, not good enough, or any of the other labels we tend to give ourselves as we grow older. So where does it all go wrong?

The fact of the matter is that we rely on those around us to teach us about the world we live in and where we fit in. In the early days, we learn from our parents, grandparents, siblings and other relatives, friends and teachers. We are conditioned by their influence and what society tells us. If we grow up in a loving, nurturing environment and are constantly told how amazing we are, then there is every possibility we'll mature into confident, positive adults. By contrast, if we grow up in a fearful environment, or are constantly being told we're not good enough, or there's not enough money to go around, or whatever negative beliefs they themselves have, then we are far more likely to grow up believing the same.

But whatever beliefs you may now have, even if you've picked up numerous negative ones, it's not necessarily the fault of anyone in particular. Laying the blame elsewhere will only serve to keep you stuck in a victim mentality and certainly not further your quest towards self-mastery and empowerment. What you have to understand is that even if your parents are behind some of your self-limiting beliefs, they were only doing the best they could, based on the beliefs that had been ingrained in them. If they were constantly coming from a place of lack or had themselves picked up the belief that money was the root of all evil, for instance, then this is what they would have taught you. Blocks to financial abundance often stem from limited beliefs we pick up from others (typically our parents) and are often linked to lack or worthiness. But the same is true for other limiting beliefs.

Not only our beliefs, but our thoughts and emotions are very much influenced by those around us too. And learning from others, called social learning, can be clearly demonstrated if we watch how a baby mirrors actions performed by those around them. The neurons in our brain responsible for this happening are actually called mirror neurons. You may already have noticed how if you're with someone and you cross your arms or legs, that they may unconsciously do the same. Or how if you yawn, this will often cause someone else to yawn too. Our mirror neurons are contagious!

The thoughts we think about most are ingrained in our implicit memory and become automatic and habitual. They are quite literally hardwired into our brain, and this is where our limiting beliefs become lodged. Whatever we tell ourself regularly enough, good or bad, will show up as our truth. These beliefs work by association and so become triggered by a particular person, event, location or anything associated with a certain memory or emotional state. While this can be very frustrating when it works against us, we have to understand that it's just our body's way of being ultra-efficient, making connections quickly so that we can interpret and then respond to our experiences accordingly.

We base all our thoughts, actions and beliefs on what we're told, or what we experience directly. We cannot know what we don't know and yet information without understanding is all but useless. When we judge something in order to reach a certain conclusion, we basically compare the unknown against what we know, reaching into the depths of our mind for answers. Most of the time we're not even aware we are doing this, but just as we judge and make assumptions, the same is happening towards us.

None of us set out to self-sabotage or create limiting beliefs. We all work with the best that we have and the cards life has dealt us up to now. But if we don't challenge our beliefs as we grow, we'll never develop personally, or spiritually. True personal growth occurs when we are open to change and willing to create new beliefs. And similar to how we came about having the beliefs in the first place, the good news is that we can work on releasing and overcoming negative ones.

> "When you change the way you look at things,
> the things you look at change."

— DR WAYNE DYER

When I look back on my life, I can easily identify patterns of self-sabotage. I started so many things and then not finished them as doubts crept in. And I could probably win awards for procrastination! Whether it was my fear of failure holding me back (if I didn't get the thing finished, or accomplish my goal then I couldn't fail could I?), or my fear of success (it can be scary to create a new future if you don't have comparisons to connect it to), or whatever excuse I was telling myself at the time, the reality was that I'd not worked on releasing my limiting beliefs.

Albert Einstein is widely credited with the quote defining insanity, saying that it's doing the same thing over and over again, but expecting different results. How many of us are guilty of this? I've reached total overwhelm and burnout on more occasions than I'd care to admit to, especially while working in office management. I repeated the same familiar pattern and then got upset when the outcome was the same. Instead of drawing on the knowledge of past experiences and challenges, I carried on as before, only working even harder. The Universe was screaming at me to listen, but I (my ego), thought it knew better! How wrong was I ...

If you are a competitive type and it took me a long time to realise I fell into this category, or are a perfectionist (also guilty), then often we can set the bar too high. It's not necessarily a bad thing to have high expectations, and I would certainly encourage you to set goals (more on this later), but unless you take care to break them down, they can quite easily end up overwhelming you. Not only that but if you don't reach your goals, you can end up feeling like you've failed which, of course, will do nothing for your self-esteem. It may also mean you're less likely to try again.

I remember being horrified when someone first suggested I had a competitive streak. As far as I was concerned, this was not a positive attribute, although in my case, it was largely against myself. I'd set massive personal goals and ridiculous targets but would then beat myself up big time if I didn't achieve them. Having said that, there have also been times when I've compared myself to others and felt lacking. Or I'd find myself getting resentful over someone else's success, especially if I felt I'd worked harder than they had and not got the results.

Just as it wasn't obvious to me I had a competitive streak, neither did I realise my own potential. Sometimes I'd be asked to do something and would automatically fall back to my default setting of doubting I could. Like when I was asked to teach a class in the karate club I belonged to. While I was already a black belt, I knew I wasn't the most senior or experienced member of the class, and I doubted my ability to do it. I remember talking to a friend about it, and she laughed. To her, it was obvious; she totally believed in me.

While it's important to acknowledge your limiting beliefs and negative self-talk, you don't need to accept them as being who you are. Your thoughts and beliefs are not YOU; they are outside of you. You can release them, and you can form new beliefs. You must be prepared to still have off days and occasions when you'll just want to scream at the world, but this is entirely normal. What you mustn't do is beat yourself up and fall into judgement mode as this will serve no one, least of all you. You have to get into the habit of acknowledging the thought for what it is and without judgement. And when you catch yourself in the act of thinking something negative, try saying the words, 'cancel, clear, delete', or simply replace the negative thought with a positive one. For example, if you catch yourself thinking you'd not be clever enough to complete a certain task, you could change the thought to, 'I am amazing and totally capable of completing …. to a high standard.'

If you find one particular negative thought crops up quite frequently, then focus on releasing it with the help of affirmations (you may like to jump to this section now in part 2). Repeating short, positive statements out loud several times a day is a great way to break a negative thought pattern. Remember that your mind doesn't know the difference between what is actually true and what it perceives to be so. It only serves to bring into your reality that which you focus on. You may also like to check out the chapter Tap To Release, also in Part 2, as emotional freedom technique (EFT) is another great tool for this.

AWARE: Are you aware of any limiting beliefs that may be holding you back? What are your thoughts around abundance, particularly money? Can you identify where these thoughts have come from and whether some (or all) of your limiting beliefs are not actually yours?

ADJUST: If you've identified any limiting beliefs, can you honestly say they're true for you NOW? Or can you adjust your mindset to see if you may have picked them up from someone else? Or if the belief was true for you as a child, but is no longer the case? If you've noticed one particular thought crops up frequently, try to catch yourself in the act and then say 'cancel, clear, delete', followed by something positive. See how this makes you feel, just by acknowledging, accepting without judgement and changing what you say to yourself.

ATTRACT: Be prepared that changing self-limiting beliefs and negative thought patterns will take time, so go easy on yourself, but equally don't be afraid to rise up for the challenge and push your boundaries. If you're serious about stepping into your secret power, it's all part of the adventure!

THE PERILS & POWER OF TIME

A really common trap you may fall into is not being present. Being too focused on living in the past, or always looking towards the future, means you'll miss out on the gift that is the present. But if you think about it this is actually the only moment in time you have any influence over, so how crazy is it if you spend so little time there? It makes no sense to dwell on matters that have passed when you can do absolutely nothing about them. Equally, while I'll go through with you the power of goal setting later in the book, if you are too focused on an end result, you'll miss the beauty of the journey.

Life is a journey to be savoured with all its ups and downs, and it is so important to slow down, breathe and smell the roses. Failure to do this is without a doubt to our detriment. Not being present sets us up to be victims of time and yet time as we know it is a human concept. Mother Nature does not follow the clock as we have been programmed to do. Life is an ever-evolving cycle of impermanence, of ebb and flow. Everything is fleeting, and we can only ever be a temporary owner of all that we think we have in life. While this concept can be scary for some, all it essentially means is that if we allow ourselves to appreciate everything and everyone in real-time, this can become a source of happiness rather than anxiety.

Think of it like this. Time as we know it is merely a convenient way to help us organise our lives and to document history, but it doesn't exist in reality. The importance of being present, on the other hand, is referenced in ancient spiritual teachings like Buddhism and also in Western psychology. One absolute certainty, however you wish to look at it, is that time is something we can never get back and yet we're often guilty of wasting far too much of it. Or we may find ourselves forever complaining we don't have enough, yet even the greatest achievers in our world have the same twenty-four hours in a day as we do. Learning and actively practising being present is something that can not only help you take control of your life but at the same time, release your very need to control it.

But that's easier said than done, right? We live in a very fast-paced world after all and have become far too eager for convenience and instant results. We try to manipulate time. From online shopping to our demand for ready meals and takeaways, to sourcing information on the internet or downloading ebooks, there is always a sense of urgency and reluctance to wait. And even then we expect faster and faster access, hence the rollout currently of 5G, the next generation of mobile internet, despite the concerns over its very safety for our health and wellbeing.

Sadly we have all but forgotten the virtue of patience and that all good things come to those who wait. Personal growth and development, along with optimal health and fitness, do not happen overnight. It is a gradual, ongoing process as we are constantly evolving, but we need to buckle up and go with it. For the sake of our own wellbeing, we can't afford to remain victims of past circumstances, nor fall into the trap of always living for tomorrow.

I have dipped in and out of both, as you may have too. So many precious moments I've wasted either stressing over things I've done or said in the past or even things I've not done and felt I should have. And don't you just love that word 'should'! It implies straight away that you don't really want to but feel obligated, or that you've already failed. Why do we do this to ourselves? And then there have been times I've properly stressed out over the future and all of the 'what-ifs?'.

Even writing this book. I've wanted to write my own book for just about as long as I can remember, but when the opportunity actually presented itself, I found myself momentarily frozen in what-if mode. What if I can't deliver? What if no one buys my book? What if no one likes my book? To which my husband replied, but what if they do!

Another example I can share is when my husband got sick. I got so caught up worrying about our future, blowing things out of proportion and fearing every possible worst-case scenario (in CBT, cognitive behavioural therapy, they refer to this as catastrophising), that I forgot to be present and grateful for the fact I had him with me at that moment. I was gripped in fear of what-if, over a situation I had absolutely no control and to make matters worse, it was robbing us both of precious moments together in the present.

When I realised what I was doing, I made a conscious effort to centre myself back in the now. However, by doing this, I found it almost unbearable to communicate with others at the time or listen to their challenges. Even close friends. And it wasn't just their challenges either. I felt unable to share their joy over other things like holidays they'd booked, or events they were looking forward to in the future when mine was so uncertain. I remember wanting to shut out the world, to jump off the merry-go-round of life and place myself and my husband in a bubble alone together. I wanted us to just be. I guess you could say I wanted to be present to the full extreme!

But then I felt guilty about wanting to shut everyone out. This wasn't me. I've always been there for others, but it's as though I suddenly found myself empty inside. I didn't have anything to give. I simply couldn't cope with anyone else's problems, nor did I want to. Most of them seemed so trivial to me at a time I was facing the biggest and most monumental challenge of my life. I felt angry that they were not tactful and sensitive to my situation. And I found it extremely hard to bite my tongue at times. I wanted to shake some of them and scream from the rooftops about how lucky they were! But of course, I knew deep inside that everyone's stress is relative. And they were only doing exactly the same as I'd been, worrying about the what-ifs of the future. But it's like I'd suddenly woken up.

Life is a miracle. Right here, right now. Think about it and look around you. While you may not necessarily have everything you want right now, the Universe has conspired to bring to you all that you need. Take a deep breath and let it out slowly. Place your hand on your heart, and feel it beating inside your chest. Rather than get caught up with the chatter inside your head, or the drama of the outside world, take a moment to just be. Not only will you experience inner peace by doing this, but it also allows you to connect to Source, raise your vibration and attract positive things into your life. All that you'll ever need is already within you. You may not have experienced your dreams outwardly yet, but the Universe is waiting to deliver if you just trust, be still and listen.

AWARE: Think about your life now. Are you aware of living largely in the past, or focusing too much on the future? How do you feel this is serving you? Chances are it is either contributing to keeping you stuck, or making you frustrated and impatient that you've not yet reached your goals. Either way, it's not likely to be bringing much peace, happiness, or sense of fulfilment to your present experience. Remember, if you are too focused on your goals and dreams, you will miss out on the journey.

ADJUST: Can you identify ways to adjust your perception of time, so that you're more able to focus on the present? An excellent way to do this is with mindfulness and meditation, so I encourage you to check out the chapter on meditation in part 2.

ATTRACT: The Universe responds to your thoughts and actions in the PRESENT, so it makes sense to spend time there! Practise being more present in your daily life and not only will you get to savour every detail of your journey, but you'll attract your every desire too.

THE STRESS CYCLE

Once you get into the habit of being more present and are prepared to acknowledge and accept, without judgement, any negative thought patterns or self-limiting beliefs that may crop up, you are already well on your way to self-mastery. With awareness comes the opportunity to create change, to form new beliefs and make more empowered choices. But you also need to consider the impact of stress. If stress is a big factor in your life and you struggle to cope day to day, then this will not serve you well or do anything for your inner peace. You seriously risk lowering your vibe, are more likely to succumb to health problems and will most certainly be on the back foot as far as manifesting your best life goes.

> "Busy is a Choice. Stress is a Choice. Joy is a Choice. Choose Well"
>
> — ANN VOSKAMP

I posted the above quote to Facebook one day with every good intention but was totally taken aback by the number of angry comments it attracted. A couple of them dared me to suggest happiness was a choice when they were going through major trauma that they certainly hadn't chosen. As I pondered over the quote and with the benefit of hindsight, I came to the conclusion that suggesting we can choose stress is perhaps not the best choice of words. But I do believe that how we react to it is firmly within our control, regardless of whether or not it feels like it.

While I consider myself a very fortunate person, I've still experienced intensely stressful periods, as I've mentioned. And at these times when everything seemed to be against me, more challenges would flood my way, until I'd find myself in a state of complete overwhelm. You know what they say, it never rains, but it pours! But it's become apparent to me over the years that I'm not alone here, with many people sharing a similar experience.

At these particularly stressful times, it seems quite commonplace to suddenly lose all logic and reason, and end up on a sort of self-sabotaging downward spiral. Can you relate to this? Regardless of whether you already know the importance of diet, meditation and having a positive mindset, it's not easy to access these tools if you neglect your self-care for too long, and are feeling totally stressed and overwhelmed. But they can all help. Of course, if you're really struggling to cope right now, I would encourage you to speak to a trustworthy friend or family member and see if they can support you at all, at least in the first instance, or seek the help of a professional.

When my husband was diagnosed with cancer, and I started drowning in fear of the what-ifs, I was well aware it was not a healthy path to be on. However, I was lucky from that respect because just by having this awareness gave me back some level of control. Not that it was easy. Just considering the fact I may need professional help made me feel weak. And when I was advised on numerous occasions by well-meaning friends to make sure I was taking care of myself, I hadn't listened. You can't pour from an empty cup I was told, and I totally knew this was true. But instead of heeding their words, I found myself getting irritated by them. Didn't they understand? How could I take time out for myself? My husband's health and wellbeing were far too important a priority, and I had to focus my time and energy on him. But it's just like when we're given the safety instructions before a flight and are told that in the event of a sudden drop in cabin pressure we must put our oxygen mask on first. If we don't and then as a consequence end up unconscious due to a lack of oxygen, we are, of course, no help to anyone! Without a doubt, I should have fitted my mask first…

The trouble is I've never been great at asking for help or accepting it if it's offered. I'm always first in line to offer support where I can to anyone else, but I've had a tendency to be pretty guarded when it comes to me. Past experiences have left me feeling let down by others, to the point I'd come to believe the only truly safe person to rely on was me. Not only is this a mistake from a spiritual point of view, because it means giving too much power to the ego at the expense of connecting to our higher self, but it's actually quite sad and lonely if we don't let others in. Vulnerability is not a weakness, as I've come to realise; it's actually a strength.

Stress means something different to everyone of course, but I think it's fair to say we typically associate it as being a negative and unavoidable part of life. We think of a stressed person as being under pressure and unable to cope, although there are some who handle stress very well and actually seem to thrive on it. For those who are influenced negatively, they may experience actual physical symptoms like headaches, insomnia, panic attacks, high blood pressure, irritable bowel syndrome and a host of other health problems, some with the potential to be life-threatening.

While often viewed as a mental or psychological problem, the term 'stress' actually refers to any upset of the natural balance of the body. It can be the result of a physical, mental or emotional stimulus and as I've already mentioned has real physical effects. Stress per se is not harmful to us, in fact, it helps to keep life interesting, but the effect of long-term, mismanaged stress is an entirely different ball game.

I don't want to bog you down with serious physiology here, but I think it's important that you have a brief understanding of how the body handles stress, aside from the mental turmoil. After all, without this natural and very physical response, we'd not have survived through the generations. Our initial immediate reaction, called the 'fight or flight' response, is geared to providing an instant energy boost and so gives us the option to run away from danger, or stand our ground and fight (as the name implies). Just some of the physiological changes that occur include the breakdown of stored glucose (sugar) to provide additional fuel, thickening of the blood in case we are injured, and the acceleration of the heart rate and breathing. Meanwhile, non-essential processes like digestion shut down, as energy is diverted away in order to power the muscles and brain.

While this fight or flight response was crucial to the prehistoric man who may have been faced with a sabre-toothed tiger, it's far more likely to be unnecessarily dramatic in modern times. Our source of stress is more likely to be mental or emotional in nature, like being stuck in traffic, work pressure, or coping with screaming children - although you may, of course, be glad of the opportunity to run away! Unfortunately, whatever the source of the stress, it will trigger the same initial response and in exactly the same way as it has always done.

Short periods of stress can be problematic. The extra release of sugar for example, intended to fuel that anticipated energy burst, is often left with nowhere to go, as our stressful situation does not require a physical response. This typically results in its conversion into fat, with weight gain around the middle closely associated with imbalanced stress hormones. However, it's long-term, poorly managed stress that wreaks the most havoc in the body.

When we are faced with periods of long-term stress, other hormones like cortisol come into play. In line with our natural bodily rhythm (called the circadian rhythm), cortisol is released at higher levels in the morning to wake us up refreshed and energised, and then tapers off as the day goes on to enable us to naturally wind down and relax in time for sleep. However, long-term stress affects this natural production and balance of cortisol, which is why poor quality sleep, be it difficulty going to sleep, restless nights, or waking in the early hours of the morning and not being able to go back to sleep, are all indicators our stress hormones may be out of balance.

Now for some good news. Aside from certain lifestyle factors that I'll cover as we journey through this book together, diet has a massive influence on our mood and mental state. Bottom line is this. The better nourished we are, the better we'll cope with stress. While it may be more challenging in the early days to pay attention to your diet, especially if you've neglected your self-care to the point of overwhelm, it's not impossible. I managed to overhaul my husband's diet and prepare and cook all our meals from scratch, using the best health-promoting foods I could lay my hands on, despite the huge stress I was under. So even if you're currently relying on caffeine, sugar and other stimulants to get you through the day and the demands placed upon you, please don't despair. In the next section, I will discuss diet and the influence it has on our body, mind and soul, and in relation to stress. Meanwhile don't be afraid to reach out to someone who can support you, whether it's emotionally, or to share your workload perhaps.

I reconnected with my Reiki family, put aside all the cancer books that were filling my every waking and sleeping hour, and got back to reading 'A Course In Miracles' instead. And yes, I did eventually have some counselling too. Being able to speak openly to someone who didn't know me and to be reassured that how I was feeling was totally normal given my situation, was worth its weight in gold. I wasn't totally losing the plot after all! And every positive step I took, however small it seemed, served to give me the confidence to reconnect to my inner power and strength. I finally accepted that while I couldn't change the circumstance that I found myself in, I could most definitely change how I responded to it. And with that came an immense sense of empowerment and inner peace.

" "God, grant me the serenity to accept the things
I cannot change, the courage to change the
things I can and the wisdom to know the
difference."

— SERENITY PRAYER, REINHOLD
NIEBUHR.

AWARE: Think about your life as it is right now. Are you
aware that stress may be playing a larger part than you'd
like? Or are you coping well? While I urge you to be
brutally honest, the idea is not to judge yourself, but just to
acknowledge if this is an area that warrants your attention.
Is it a case of having to accept that your current situation is
out of your control as I had to? Or are there changes that
can be made? Use the simple but powerful prayer above to
tap into the power of the Creator and ask for the necessary
wisdom to guide you.

ADJUST: Remember, you're not looking to get rid of stress
entirely, but just to identify whether there are any adjustments you can make to actively reduce it. Can you identify
individual stressors or one main issue that you could work
towards improving? Make a note of them and brainstorm
possible action steps. Don't overthink and don't worry
whether or not it will be easy to take the steps, as I merely
want you to expand your thinking at this point.

<u>ATTRACT</u>: By consciously thinking about the changes you'd like to make, the Universe will conspire to make them happen. There's no need for you to stress further by concerning yourself with the details, just be open to attract the best possible outcome. But one word of caution. Be sure NOT to focus on the negatives and the chaos in your life, as this will only bring you more of the same! Take a deep breath and trust that all will be well.

PART 2 - ADJUST TO ALLOW

THE NUTRITION CONNECTION

In the previous section, I explained some of the reasons we self-sabotage and how fear, limiting beliefs and negative thought patterns can keep us stuck. We also looked at the impact of stress and how it can further compound our problems, and I asked you to start thinking about the changes you'd like to see in your life and to identify where adjustments could be made. Now it's time to delve into this in more detail because once you've acknowledged and accepted where you're at and can identify what adjustments are necessary, you put yourself in a very empowering position. You give yourself the gift of choice. And once you make the commitment to move forwards and take positive action towards creating change, you really step into your power. You show the Universe you mean business and this, in turn, will set you up to ALLOW all the things you desire into your life.

In this section, I'll introduce you to specific tools and techniques you can use straight away to help with adjustments to your diet, and for your mindset and spiritual growth. I'll start by exploring ways to nourish your body and mind with food because diet has an extremely important role to play and is often neglected in self-empowerment books. I'm not saying you can't improve your mindset or develop spiritually if you eat rubbish, or necessarily that you won't feel fit and well, but if this is an area you're neglecting at the moment just think of the potential if you fixed this too?

As I've already mentioned, this is where my journey really began. After suffering from postnatal depression and feeling totally worthless, nutrition was my salvation in more ways than one. But even long before this, I'd had an interest in complementary therapies. I'd suffered badly with teenage acne, which had massively affected my confidence and caused me to lose faith in conventional medicine. While I was told by my GP at the time that diet had no influence on the health of the skin, I wasn't so sure and had a nagging feeling inside that this didn't make sense. Our skin is the largest organ of elimination after all, so if the liver is struggling to break down toxins, they can easily be excreted via the skin.

Not that I really thought a toxic system was to blame for my acne at the time. I suspected more of a hormonal link. But if you really think about it, it doesn't seem beyond the realms of possibility that our diet can affect everything that goes on within the body. Conventional medicine has finally accepted as fact the influence it has on blood sugar and now gives diet advice to diabetics, and likewise how essential a healthy diet is in the fight against cancer and heart disease. So why should it be any different for our health and well-being generally? And not just our physical body. It has far, far wider-reaching effects, as I've come to understand in more recent years. Diet has a massive influence on our vibration. But more on that later...

Let's start with our mental and physical health. Our brain depends on a second by second supply of nutrients to process and maintain all our body functions. Whether it's making antibodies for our immune system or enzymes to break down our food, producing hormones, or for cell growth and repair, vital nutrients are involved in every step of the way. And nutrient deficiencies, even in the so-called civilised West, are rampant due to modern farming practices, artificial ripening or long-term storage of fresh foods and our processed, high sugar diet. Alongside this, we have to deal with environmental pollution, and a multitude of artificial chemicals and sweeteners now thought of as the norm in our food. In fact, scientists estimate that by following the standard Western diet, we could be eating in excess of forty unnatural chemicals at each meal! If on top of this, we regularly consume deep-fried, burnt or barbecued food, drink copious quantities of alcohol, or take recreational or prescription drugs, then we further add to our toxic burden. Why do we put our body under so much pressure and then expect to get the best out of it?

Just imagine you were the proud owner of a brand spanking new high-performance racing car and you wanted it to win the Formula 1, would you chance filling it up with inferior grade fuel? Of course not! You would understand the necessity of using the best fuel available to you to give you every chance of optimising its performance. And I have no doubt you'd make sure to have it serviced and maintained to the best of your ability too! So why treat your body any differently? If your diet lacks nutrients, then it's like putting inferior fuel in your car, which means you'll be far less likely to be firing on all cylinders. If you want to optimise your performance physically, mentally and spiritually, then you need to fill up with premium-grade fuel.

Before I get into some general dietary guidelines, I do just want to clarify something. You need to understand that the saying 'you are what you eat', is not entirely accurate. It's more like 'you are what you digest and absorb'. Remember when I told you I suffered from teenage acne? Well, much to my despair, this turned into aggressive adult acne. In fact, it continued well into my nutritional therapy training. I can remember washing my face of cover-up makeup one evening as my husband came into the bathroom and I broke down. 'Who is going to take me seriously as a nutritional therapist with a face like this?' I remember asking him, as the tears streamed down my face. As far as I was concerned, I was doing everything I possibly could, my diet was amazing, and I was taking several quality nutritional supplements, but my skin just wasn't improving.

Aside from my low self-esteem and poor mental state at the time, both of which I now know would have had a massive bearing on my healing, it also turned out that I had a leaky gut. I won't go into that here, but suffice to say that a combination of factors had caused my gut to become more permeable than it's meant to be, which then affected how efficiently I was able to absorb nutrients. While my healthy diet and supplements would have helped to some degree, my inability to absorb key vitamins, minerals and other nutrients would also have resulted in very expensive urine!

I felt it was important to share this, as I know how frustrating it can be when you work hard to make positive changes, with diet or whatever, and then don't experience results. Of course, there is an element of time involved, and some may give up too soon, and as I've already mentioned, change takes time. Even when you add in therapeutic levels of supplements to bring about balance and healing in the body, you must remember they are not medicinal drugs and will likely take longer to work. They'll correct underlying nutritional deficiencies first that may go unnoticed, but will be vitally important nevertheless and contribute to more obvious changes over time.

And then there are other factors to take into consideration like when you eat and under what circumstances, and even whether or not you chew your food properly. Certain factors are detrimental to digestion, for example, eating too late in the evening or when tired or stressed. Stress can actually shut down the digestive process, which is why it's so closely linked to health problems like irritable bowel syndrome (IBS). Remember the stress response is a very physical one as I've already explained and is geared up to help you react to a threat in an instant. If you were to suddenly find yourself faced with that sabre-toothed tiger (OK, so that's not likely to happen), let's say you step out in front of a car, your body will NOT be worrying at that point about digesting your lunch!

But with all that said, your diet should form the basic foundation from which to optimise your overall health and wellbeing, so let's take a look at what this means in practical terms. While healthy eating is largely common sense, it does mean different things to different people and across different cultures, spiritual practices or beliefs too. Chinese and Indian healing systems completely contradict each other for a start. Hindus are totally against eating meat and consider it a sin, while in Chinese culture, it is recommended as part of a balanced and healing diet.

There is so much conflicting information out there, even across a single culture, that it can be difficult to know where to start. Even with my background in nutritional therapy, I'm not embarrassed to admit I found it completely overwhelming when I began researching the best and most up to date diet for my husband's specific form of cancer. It was mind-blowing—everything from strict vegan to Keto, which is practically at the other end of the spectrum. I followed my instinct in the end, but knew at the same time; I had to respect my husband's degree of compliance! At the end of the day, whatever diet you choose, it has to be doable.

Over the years, I've followed no end of different healthy diets, searching for the nutritional version of the Holy Grail. From Eat Right For Your Blood Type to Paleo and even vegan (and many in-between). My conclusion over this time is that there's simply no such thing as a one diet fits all. We are all unique individuals, and apart from anything else, each has varying requirements for nutrients and calories. A growing child, for example, will need far more of both than an elderly, sedentary person. This means that while I will be giving you nutritional tips and also make you aware of which foods help to raise your vibration, it'll largely be down to you and some trial and error, to find what makes YOU feel healthy, vibrant and alive. What I can tell you though is that the more in tune you become with your body, the more you'll instinctively be drawn to make healthier choices. You just have to listen.

I need you to bear in mind that a lot of our current dietary advice is outdated. For a start, we have become very fat-phobic. And yet, despite all the low-fat guidelines that are consistently thrown at us, the incidence of obesity, diabetes and heart disease continues to soar. It's so important to realise there are good and bad fats, and that even some saturated fat (yes, there are healthy options), is crucial to us.

So going back to my earlier question, how do we even know what constitutes a healthy diet? Should we judge it by how much fat is in our food, or sugar, or how many calories it contains? Or should we consider other factors?

I think it's fair to say that most of us would appreciate that a diet rich in processed, refined foods, takeaways and ready meals would not be considered healthy. This 'diet' will not only be typically low in essential nutrients but high in sugar, salt and bad fats. Worse still, it will likely be laced with chemical additives and preservatives, giving your body a mammoth task trying to break it all down. Not only will this have potential health implications, but it will also have a detrimental effect on your weight and your mood. Food is addictive and sugar especially, and the food industry has utilised this knowledge to their best advantage...

This is why it is so important to optimise your diet and the principle behind it is simple. You should choose to eat food as close to its natural state as possible. This means increasing raw and lightly steamed vegetables, fresh fruits, quality protein (like grass-fed meat, poultry, fish and eggs – or vegetarian sources like quinoa, pulses and avocado), and essential fats from nuts, seeds and their cold-pressed oils. Staying optimally hydrated is also key, ideally drinking fresh, filtered water, or herbal teas. And I'd encourage as much variety as possible, as this ensures a wide intake of nutrients and helps prevent susceptibility to food intolerances.

When you follow a diet full of fresh, natural whole foods, your body will easily be able to break down the various components. These include fats, carbohydrates, proteins, vitamins and minerals, which your body will then be able to make immediate use of. These breakdown products are used for the smooth and efficient running of all processes of the body, meaning you will be far more likely to benefit from a healthy metabolism, balanced hormones, efficient digestion etc. By contrast, if you eat processed foods not only are they empty calories in themselves, meaning they'll not provide you with any nutritional value, but they'll also rob you of vital nutrients, as your body struggles to recognise the various components and break them down. In the next section , I want to explore this in a little more detail.

EATING FOR HEALTH & VITALITY

You now know the major role our diet has to play for us to achieve optimal health and vitality, but what I haven't yet shared is how even the slightest improvements can be beneficial. I actually encourage you to take small steps, especially if you have identified the need to make some pretty major dietary changes over time. Not only will this allow your body to get used to new foods and help reduce the risk of you suffering withdrawal symptoms as you remove others, but it will also improve your chances of sticking with it long-term. This is what we're after; not a 'diet' with a start and end date, but a diet for life. I have repeatedly found with my nutrition clients that the more strict and rigid their diet, however eager they are to create positive change in the shortest time possible, only sets them up for failure long-term. None of us likes to feel deprived, and if you deny yourself every single treat, this is not ideal to guarantee your compliance for the long haul.

Take your time, go easy on yourself, don't beat yourself up if you make an unhealthy food choice now and again, and don't be disheartened if you don't notice improvements overnight. That said, I have known many people change their diet and notice positive changes in as little as two weeks, particularly where mood and energy levels are concerned. Remember, your diet provides that all-important fuel for your body. Choose wisely and you'll be happy, healthy, energised, and feel empowered and motivated to go after your goals. Choose poorly and you'll be prone to colds and infections, feel drowsy and sluggish during the day, and suffer more with irritability and mood swings. Not conducive to you living your best life!

Blood Sugar - A Delicate Balancing Act

Once again, while I don't want to get too caught up in the science, it's important you're aware of how big an influence your blood sugar has to your optimal wellbeing. I'm not referring to diabetes here, just normal blood sugar dips and troughs throughout the day. Apart from low energy levels and mood, imbalanced blood sugar may contribute to a host of other symptoms like poor memory and concentration, headaches, insomnia, weight problems, cravings and depression.

Diet massively affects our ability to balance blood sugar optimally, along with other factors like stress. Without any exaggeration, I would estimate that well over 80% (and probably nearer 90%) of all clients I see present with a mild to moderate blood sugar imbalance. Why? The standard refined and high sugar Western diet, along with our reliance on stimulants like coffee, tea and cola drinks is largely to blame, but I firmly believe it has a lot to do with the fast-paced lifestyle we typically now lead too. We're always rushing about, eating on the run, juggling work with home and family life. We never stop to take a breath. Can you relate to this?

Stress affects blood sugar and depletes us of nutrients, while diet can massively help support blood sugar and how we cope with stress. Similarly, moderate exercise can help balance blood sugar and relieve stress, while training excessively adds to the stress burden and is detrimental. But let's focus on the diet.

While the jury remains out as to whether they are the best fuel source, carbohydrates are undoubtedly the preferred fuel for the body. We typically think of our carbohydrate foods as being potatoes, pasta, bread, rice, cereals and grains, but these are just our starchy carbohydrates. Also included are our fruits and vegetables. All carbohydrates are broken down into glucose (sugar) and therefore cause our blood sugar levels to go up when they are eaten. Your body then converts this excess blood glucose into energy as it's required, or stores it as fat.

It's important to understand that not all carbohydrates are created equal. They may help improve our energy levels and mood, or have the complete reverse effect and influence them negatively. Fibrous leafy green vegetables like broccoli, kale and cabbage are generally considered to be our best sources of complex carbohydrates, followed by other vegetables and then fruit. While fruit provides a rich source of nutrients, especially our all-important antioxidant nutrients, it's worth bearing in mind that it is high in sugar too. And as this is typically released fairly rapidly, I wouldn't recommend you gorge on fruit, despite its health benefits, but limit portions to one or two a day.

If you take a look at the very outdated food pyramid, it recommends we base our entire diet around starchy carbohydrate foods. And it's still widely accepted that cereals and grains of the whole variety (like porridge oats, brown rice and wholemeal bread), are good sources of carbohydrate. However, more recent research suggests we'd all do better avoiding these particular foods, which is where the Paleo, Keto and No Grain diets have sprung from. One of the points they raise is that burning fat for fuel, rather than carbohydrate, is much better for us. Having read the research, I am a fan of these diets, but I suggest you judge them on your own merit.

So just to recap, all carbohydrate foods break down into glucose, but the more fibrous and complex they are, the slower they'll release this. These are the ones I'd recommend you include in your diet. Those to avoid are the refined white foods, like white bread and white rice, and also cakes, biscuits, chocolate, confectionery and soda drinks. Don't be fooled into thinking you need these sugary foods for energy. In actual fact, because they break down into glucose very rapidly, they'll cause a sudden spike in blood sugar, and while this may provide a short energy burst for you, it's not lasting. Worse still, as your body frantically tries to restore balance, it will overcompensate, which will result in a crash as blood glucose plummets.

At this stage not only will your energy levels drop, but you may also experience symptoms I mentioned earlier like headaches, anxiety, feeling faint or shaking. Plus, you're likely to crave more of the same problems foods (or stimulants like coffee) and find yourself in a vicious cycle. It's worth mentioning again that refined foods are basically empty calories as they lack nutrients, like the all-important B vitamins, which essential for our entire metabolic process. And this doesn't just affect our energy, but all the chemical reactions that occur in our body. Also, a high sugar diet massively lowers our immune response.

Don't be fooled into thinking the no sugar versions are any better for you, because they're not! Artificial sweeteners not only carry dubious health concerns of their own, but they can still affect your blood sugar over time. The only alternative sweeteners that are acceptable in my view are Xylitol and Stevia, although I do use just a little coconut sugar on the odd occasion too. Ideally cut out all the added sugar in your diet, which may be difficult at first, so do this gradually, but your body will thank you for it, and you will eventually lose your sweet tooth.

Food Intolerances

Our vital energy and indeed mental state can also be affected by food intolerances. Not the same as classic allergies they can be hard to identify, but ironically we often crave problem foods, and so this may provide a clue. By contrast, someone who suffers from a classic food allergy like a peanut allergy is almost certainly aware of it, due to the sometimes life-threatening consequences of eating it. They have to avoid the allergic food for life. But the person who suffers from a food intolerance may be blissfully unaware. Or they may suffer from low-grade energy and a range of other niggling symptoms like dark circles under the eyes, constipation, wind and bloating. Common problem foods as far as food intolerances are concerned include wheat and dairy products.

If you suspect you may have a food intolerance or multiple intolerances, I'd recommend you seek the help of a nutritional therapist or at least research into this further. It's far too complex a topic for me to address properly here. There are tests around to help identify them, but be aware that some are as good as useless and may give false positive or negative results. Another thing to bear in mind is that even if you do identify intolerances, this is likely just a piece of a larger puzzle. You may have a leaky gut as I did and if no consideration is given to heal this, simply removing problem foods from your diet may provide only temporary relief, before you then start reacting to other foods. And this carries the very real risk of your diet becoming more and more restrictive and you suffering from multiple nutritional deficiencies. This is not going to be conducive to you feeling on top of the world, vibrant and alive!

The best I can suggest here is that if you suspect a single food intolerance, then you could follow a trial elimination. Remove the food from your diet for a couple of weeks, while keeping a food diary and record not only everything you eat but any symptoms you may experience or what you notice improve during that time. Pay particular attention to symptoms like bloating, and also your mood and energy levels. When the two weeks are up, you should gradually reintroduce the food, once again paying close attention to any change or return of symptoms. I recommend you avoid going it alone with strict elimination diets of multiple foods, as this should only be undertaken under professional guidance and supervision.

Our Second Brain

There are so many examples I could give of where diet impacts our health, but for the purposes of this book, I need to move on. However, I can't finish this chapter without mentioning the health of the gut generally, as it has such a bearing on overall wellbeing. Unless you suffer from digestive problems already it's perhaps unlikely you've given it much thought and yet it may surprise you to learn that our gut is often referred to as the second brain. And you've guessed it; the diet has a massive influence. Eat a high sugar, processed, high meat diet, and you risk no end of problems, plus your body will almost certainly be in a highly inflammatory state. In fact, it's believed that most, if not all inflammatory conditions stem from the gut, while health problems like autism also have a strong link.

If on the other hand, you choose to base your diet around healthy, fibrous whole foods, fruits and veggies, it'll not only help to keep you regular and so effectively eliminate toxins from the body, but it will also help your immune system, support hormone balance and nourish your microbiome (your healthy gut flora). Add in some natural, live yoghurt along with fermented foods like sauerkraut, and this can further help to improve the environment within your gut, as can taking a probiotic supplement (which contain beneficial bacteria to help repopulate your bowel).

I hope this has helped you understand the key role diet has to play to optimise your wellbeing, but don't get too hung up on it. My intention is not that you worry about everything that goes into your mouth, and you become paranoid about reading food labels. Moderation is key at the end of the day. I often suggest you think of your diet like a bank balance. All the healthy foods you consume are like putting deposits into the bank, while the odd takeaway or processed meal, pudding or pastry is like taking a withdrawal out. Provided your deposits are greater than your withdrawals; your body should cope quite satisfactorily. You'll likely find that once you become more in tune with your body and align with your higher self, you will instinctively be drawn to foods that are better for you anyway. Let me summarise with a few general tips.

Foods to limit in your diet:

Limit high sugar snacks, caffeine, fizzy drinks, alcohol and refined/processed foods (empty calories). Also limit processed meats of any kind, hamburgers, chips and other fast foods, fried foods, crisps and high-fat foods like standard supermarket-bought meat, sausages, sausage rolls, pies and pasties. This doesn't mean you can't have them, coffee, chocolate and alcohol have known health benefits in moderation, but this is the key!

∾

Foods to include in your diet:

Remember that variety is important to ensure a wide range of nutrients and to help prevent susceptibility to food intolerances:

- Carbohydrates - for energy and B vitamins – green leafy vegetables, avocado, sweet potato and, if eating grains, wholemeal bread, brown rice, wholemeal pasta, oats, millet.
- Protein - (combine with carbohydrates for best blood sugar support); oily fish (e.g. tuna, trout, mackerel, sardines, salmon), white fish (e.g. cod, plaice, haddock), poultry (chicken, turkey), eggs, lean meat, cheese and/or vegetarian protein (e.g. beans, peas, lentils, Quorn, quinoa, tofu, jackfruit, nuts, seeds, humous, avocado). If you eat fish, then buy wild where you can (e.g. wild Alaskan salmon), and for meat, I would recommend you choose grass-fed. Grass-fed meat is by far superior and has less total fat, saturated fat, cholesterol and calories to the standard supermarket meat. It also has more vitamin A, C and E, and a number of health-promoting fats, including omega-3 fatty acids and CLA (shown to help reduce abdominal fat). This is meat as nature intended it, where cows eat GRASS and not grain. If you can't find this, then at the very least opt for free-range or organic.
- Essential Fats – found in oily fish, nuts (almonds,

Brazils, walnuts -not roasted or salted), seeds (pumpkin, sunflower, hemp sesame and linseeds, and their cold-pressed oils that may be used as a salad dressing or mixed into smoothies.) Avoid cooking with essential fats as heat damages them, and ideally store nuts and seeds in the fridge in an airtight container. Essential fats enhance energy production, promote hormone balance, improve mental function and are essential for the very structure of our cell membranes. Saturated fats, on the other hand, from meat and dairy products (like milk and cheese), are not essential and can make you sluggish.

- Fruit & Vegetables - a source of carbohydrate for energy and contain many essential vitamins and minerals for optimal health and vitality – aim for 2 portions of fruit and an absolute minimum of 5 portions of varied vegetables daily (not including potatoes).

- Water - essential for life itself. Dehydration can lower energy levels and lead to aches and pains in the body, among other things. Aim for 6-8 glasses daily (1-1.5 litres). Also try fruit/herb teas or Rooibos tea (native South African tea that is naturally caffeine-free), or a slice of lemon in hot water which is very refreshing!

MINDSET & FOOD - RAISING YOUR VIBE!

OK, so you now understand how important our diet is from a functional point of view and how the breakdown components from our food form the building blocks for what goes on within our body and mind, but now let's take a look from a spiritual perspective. And once again it's all a matter of vibration.

I've already explained how each and every one of us is a unique, energetic being, and we live in a vibrational universe where everything is connected. As someone who practices Reiki, I am also familiar with the term 'life force energy' and am comfortable in the knowledge it's at the very core of each and every one of us. It's who we are. Reiki comes from the Japanese words Rei (meaning universal) and Ki (life energy), so roughly translates as universal, or spiritually guided, life force energy. But you don't have to have any knowledge of Reiki to appreciate or understand how vital our life force energy is and that it requires as much consideration, if not more, than our physical body.

Not that I've always accepted this. In fact, as I've already told you when I first qualified in nutritional therapy, I was still quite closed-minded and would have been far too skeptical of energy healing, or the suggestion of life force energy. But it's only because, like many of us, I didn't know any better.

In our Western culture, we are simply not taught such a thing even exists. If we get ill, we only recognise the physical manifestation of the illness. As a complementary therapist, I've always known the importance of treating the whole body to promote natural balance and healing, as opposed to just focusing on presenting symptoms, but I had no knowledge of our energetic potential and how it could affect us. Western medicine has no term or understanding of life force energy, and so it seems an alien concept to us when we come across it.

But it's not only the Japanese who hold in high regard this extremely vital part of us; in fact, many Eastern cultures do. In China, our life force energy is referred to as Chi and in India, Prana. They readily accept we are six sensory beings, but in the West, we only recognise the five physical senses (sight, taste, touch, hearing and smell). If we have a strong life force energy, we are happy, vital, and love life, but if our life force is depleted, we can become withdrawn, depressed and manifest physical symptoms and disease.

One way we can raise our life force energy and align more favourably with our spirit is to base our diet around nourishing, high vibration foods. Now, this doesn't mean to say that if you live on organic green juices alone that you'll definitely reach the path of spiritual enlightenment, but it will help! However on the flip side, even if you eat the best healthy raw food, organic, vegan diet possible, but fail to work on clearing old limiting beliefs, doubts, fears or other negative thought patterns, you're still likely to feel blocked on your spiritual path.

But let's stick with the diet for now. Eating a largely plant-based diet rich not only in nutrients but in lifeforce energy has been shown to improve our perception by nourishing our pineal gland and third eye chakra. In fact, when we feel good, our energetic vibration increases and activates not only our upper chakras but creates better flow in all seven of our major energy centres. This helps us connect to our spiritual centre. (If you're not familiar with chakras then to put it very simply they are the energy centres in our body.)

The Acid / Alkaline Balance

A large proportion of what we eat is acid-forming. Apart from having many negative health implications, it also causes calcium to be leached out of our bones in an attempt to neutralise the acid. Acidic foods include meat and dairy foods, eggs, refined and processed foods, most cereals and grains, sugar, coffee and alcohol. These foods are more energy consuming to break down and digest and increase the risk of inflammation in the body. They also reduce the energy available to our third eye and crown chakras, so make it harder for us to connect spiritually.

By contrast, our fruits and vegetables are very alkalising and hugely beneficial for the body. They help raise our energetic frequency to more effectively connect to the upper chakras. Even citrus fruit, like lemons that we might typically associate with being highly acidic, are actually very alkaline once they are broken down in the body. Likewise, some grains are more alkaline like millet and quinoa (which is actually a protein-rich seed), nuts like almonds and cashews, and seeds like hemp and chia.

Our Essential Fats

When we think of food from a vibrational perspective, we mustn't forget the healthy fats. Another reason not to fall into the trap of becoming fat-phobic is that our healthy, plant-based fats are essential components to a spiritually motivated diet. Of particular importance are our Omega 3 essential fats, obtained largely from oily fish like salmon or sardines but also found in hemp, blackcurrant and linseeds, and then our Omega 6 fats from most other nuts and seeds. These essential fats cannot be made in the body and so, as their name suggests, are essential to include in the diet. Although our requirement for Omega 6 is greater, it is generally more readily available in the diet. For this reason, it makes sense to focus our attention on ensuring a plentiful supply of Omega 3 essential oils.

Last but most certainly not least are other very healthy fats. Not considered essential in quite the same way, but are definitely recommended to include in the diet and come from olives and extra virgin olive oil, virgin coconut oil, and avocados. While coconut oil is actually a saturated fat, which makes some people reluctant to add it to their diet, it's important to understand it is naturally occurring and not artificially manipulated. Apart from helping to raise your vibe, it carries a whole host of other amazing health benefits too.

Should We Eat Animal Protein?

As far as spirituality is concerned, there is always a debate over whether or not we should eat animal protein. I've already mentioned how different cultures hold different beliefs over this, and so I think it's important to leave this decision up to you. That said, and because meat and dairy foods are more mucous forming and energy-consuming to breakdown, I would encourage you to be mindful of how much you include them in your diet. At the very least, I'd recommend you choose grass-fed or organic wherever possible, as not only are the animals treated more humanely, but they are not pumped full of growth hormones, antibiotics and other drugs like the majority of standard supermarket meat. You may find that the more you raise your vibration, the more sensitive you become to lower vibrational foods and will naturally move away from them - but don't feel bad if you don't!

If you're really serious about transitioning to a high vibe diet, then it's my belief you should change the way you look at food, just as much as changing the actual foods themselves. Savour and enjoy your food, by bringing in the social element too, but also view it as medicine and not just fuel. You can get fuel from a sugar-laden doughnut, but it's not going to provide any worthwhile nutrition or raise your vibration. And while it may make you feel good at the time, it'll probably lower your mood in the long run, especially if you consider what it may have done to your waistline!

But as I've said before, it's all about balance. Don't feel guilty about the way you're eating now, but shift your awareness towards making healthier choices for the benefit of your body, mind and spirit. If you eat low vibrational foods and this is your choice after all, or just have the odd blip, don't then get into a state of judgement. It's just not worth it, especially as by doing this you'll be compounding the negative effects. Your thoughts are vibrational in nature too remember, so never underestimate the power of the mind. You'd be far better served to bless the low vibration food with love and gratitude. This act in itself if carried out sincerely will help to improve its vibration, although don't be fooled into using this all the time as a get out of jail free card!

While I'm on the subject of blessing our food, this really has been shown to have a massive effect on raising its vibration. Some research has identified it as having the ability to change the very structure of food and water particles. Other high vibe practices that have been used around food with similar effects include Reiki, crystals and magnetic therapy.

And so to summarise this section, ideally anything unnatural should be avoided in your diet. The more consistently you choose healthy food options and become better in tune with your body, the more you will naturally desire them.

And the reward will not only be better health, but a more uplifted mood and higher vibration, and ultimately a deeper connection to your higher self. I mentioned before how the saying 'you are what you eat' is not entirely accurate, because if we're not absorbing nutrients efficiently, this will hinder even a healthy diet, but so will a negative mindset or low vibrational state. We are what we eat to some degree, of course, but we're also very much what we think, say, believe and do.

On that note, it's important to understand how your diet can become fear-based, and this will not serve you. If you optimise your diet for the right reasons, to improve your overall wellbeing, then this is great. But if you fear everything you eat and are paranoid it will cause ill health if you deviate from your very strict regime, then this will deplete your life force energy and can bring on the very thing you are worried about getting.

In her book 'Dying To Be Me', Anita Moorjani explains how this happened to her. Paranoid about getting cancer, she switched to a rigid organic, vegan diet, avoided all toxic toiletries and did everything she possibly could to steer clear of the disease. But her choices were very much based on fear which depletes life force energy. She also spent all her time focusing on cancer and the fact it was about NOT getting it was irrelevant to what the Universe heard. And so you've guessed it, she ended up getting cancer, which is a fear-based diagnosis in itself.

So what raises our life force energy, aside from eating nourishing foods? Simple. Everything related to love, and this very much includes loving, accepting and appreciating yourself and where you are right now. Sound like a broken record? Sorry, but it's true! Everything has to start with you. But also be sure to spend time with the people you love and who lift you up, who you can laugh and have a great time with. Being out in nature, spending time with animals, connecting with your angels and getting adequate sleep are other great ways to raise your vibe, and of course, you may like to try a healing modality like Reiki. Simply put; your life force energy is strengthened by your loving connection with yourself and others. Don't neglect it!

If you'd like to read more about diet from a spiritual perspective, then I would encourage you to read 'Life Changing Foods' by the Medical Medium, Anthony William.

AWARE: Has this section made you more aware of the power of nutrition and how you can manipulate your diet to serve you? And equally how it can hinder your efforts to fire on all cylinders and grow spiritually if you don't get it quite right, or if there are underlying issues that need to be addressed? Has it made you think about your relationship with food? Are you able to accept where you are without judgement and understand it's not about getting it right 100% of the time? Remember, mindset plays a big part with your food choices.

ADJUST: Have you been able to identify any changes you can make to ensure you're topping up with premium-grade fuel? Perhaps you can get into the habit of eating more fruit and vegetables, or drinking more water as a first step? Or start cutting down on sugar, processed foods, or stimulants? Remember to implement any changes gradually!

ATTRACT: By focusing on healthier food options, you'll be nourishing your body, mind and soul, which will help to transform you from the inside out. Provided you make the changes for the right reasons and not through fear, you'll raise your vibration and life force energy, feel empowered and motivated to live life to the full and attract no end of miracles into your life!

THE GRAVITY OF GRATITUDE

Moving on from diet, I now want to introduce you to other techniques and practices that will further impact your life force energy and raise your vibration. And there's nothing more powerful in my opinion, than the practice of gratitude. Not only will you raise your own vibration when you express gratitude, but you'll shift the energy around you to a higher frequency too. It's almost as though you become a human magnet, drawing good things and people into your experience. They naturally gravitate towards you, as you are like a beacon that emanates positive energy and apart from anything else this makes you a joy to be around. I'm sure you will have noticed how an attitude of gratitude is very attractive to us, so don't be fooled by the simplicity of the words 'thank you'. The Universe and your angels will rejoice every time you give thanks.

'Always be grateful for what you have, you'll end up having more ...'

But let's face it, it's much easier to express gratitude when everything is rosy and working out, as opposed to when it's not, but you may be surprised to hear that it's during the challenging times when it's even more important to find something to be thankful for, however small that something may be. That said, many of us can be guilty of neglecting to express gratitude even when great things are manifesting, so it's definitely something we all need to practice! In a society driven by consumerism where we're constantly reminded of what we don't have but definitely 'need', it's all too easy to be ungrateful and fall into the trap of always wanting more. And if we're working tirelessly towards goals that always seem to evade us, or have suffered a crisis, emotional, financial or otherwise, gratitude can be a bitter pill to swallow.

The trouble is, once we find ourselves trapped in victim mentality, we can't see the wood for the trees. We tend only to notice what isn't working out and blame everyone or everything else. I speak from experience. What is essential to understand though, is that becoming all consumed by the bad stuff will not bring about positive change, and it makes it all the more difficult to appreciate anything good. It's like a vicious circle. But what I've come to realise is that there's always something to be thankful for. Always.

In actual fact, it's at those times when things aren't working out, and you feel as though your world is crashing down around you that gratitude must take centre stage, however hard. Why? Because it's the surest route to raising your vibration and achieving the outcome and happiness you deserve. It's because of your challenges and perceived failures that you have the opportunity to take a step back and view the situation from a different perspective. Redirecting your focus and taking stock of all the good in your life puts you back in the driving seat and is essential for you to move forwards.

If you're still not convinced or feel able to offer gratitude, especially if you're currently going through a difficult time, look at it this way. Not only is it respectful to say thank you for what you currently have in your life (or simply for the fact you are alive), but by redirecting your focus to something positive you will send a message out loud and clear to the Universe that you want more of it. Remember, where your attention and focus goes, your energy flows, or to put it another way, you get what you focus on. If you only ever focus on all the bad in your life, then it's a pretty foregone conclusion that you'll end up with more of the same.

Think about it. Have you noticed similar negative patterns keep repeating themselves? Maybe you've noticed you only ever seem to attract nasty, abusive partners? Or perhaps you've had a bad experience at work and changed your job, as I did several times, only to find a similar scenario unfolds with the new one. If you want your life to change, if you're after better, more positive experiences and outcomes, then it's essential you get into the habit of being thankful.

66 "By feeling grateful, we let God in. Then we're connected to love, and as miracles occur naturally as expressions of love, our prayers will begin to be answered."

— KYLE GRAY, ANGEL PRAYERS.

Keeping a gratitude journal is a great way to get into the habit of expressing thanks. As soon as you wake up in the morning write down 3-5 things you are grateful for. If you struggle with this number, then write less, but be sure to note at least one thing. And 'feel' into it. It's no good just writing random things for the sake of it if they don't feel sincere to you. By doing this first thing in the morning, it will raise your vibration and help set your intention and mindset for a good day.

I'd also suggest you repeat the exercise just before you go to bed. Think back to what happened during the day and write down another 3-5 things you can be grateful for. Remember not to focus on any negatives. If the day didn't go as well as you'd have liked you may have to think a little harder, but I can assure you there will be something you can be grateful for, even if it's just that you managed to get through the day. Don't hone in on what you could have done better, what you didn't achieve or your ever-growing to-do list so that your mind is in turmoil before you attempt to sleep. By choosing to express gratitude instead you'll not only lift your vibration, hugely raising your ability to become a manifestation magnet, but you'll also give yourself a much better chance of enjoying a restful night's sleep!

If you don't like the idea of keeping a written journal, there are other options, like Apps you can download to your phone that will prompt you to keep track of what you're grateful for. Or you can voice record a list on your phone, giving you the option to offer thanks in real-time throughout the day, as soon as you notice something positive and then play it back before you go to bed. Whichever method you choose, I encourage you to stick with it for at least 21 days, as it takes about this length of time to form a habit.

Of course, there are many ways you can express gratitude and saying thank you to others should become as natural to you as breathing. It need not cost a thing, although if you're not able to thank someone in person, you could post them a thank you note later, or send them some flowers or a small gift. And if you don't have anything specifically to thank them for then why not just say a few kind words or pay them a compliment? Don't underestimate the power this will have to brighten someone's day. Similarly, why not pick up the phone and call someone, and really listen with all your attention when they speak to you, or just send a quick message to let them know they are in your thoughts. Simple acts of kindness and appreciation that cost nothing, yet have the potential to yield countless benefits.

And it is worth the effort. Transformational shifts really can occur when you express your gratitude sincerely, and this is the key as I've already mentioned.

Now I'll be brutally honest with you here; this wasn't the easiest chapter to write. In fact, it was just as I was about halfway through it that I received the devastating news about my husband's cancer. Was it easy to be grateful? Hell no! I've already told you how I got through those early days and weeks on auto-pilot, and very much from a place of fear. However once I'd had time to get over the initial shock and while I'm not going to lie, I'd rather he'd never had the diagnosis in the first place, I still knew there was so much to be grateful for.

My husband was fast-tracked for the tests he needed due to his younger age, and even despite the cancer diagnosis, it was not of the type his consultant had initially feared. Plus, I had the nutritional knowledge to be able to fully optimise his diet and was able to offer him Reiki healing and tap into other complementary therapies. I was also extremely grateful for my husband's amazingly positive attitude, and for the friends and family who supported us throughout. And now I can add, as I review this chapter as part of my final manuscript, how intensely grateful I am that my husband has just been told he's in full and complete remission! Without a doubt, gratitude adds so much power to our prayers.

So no, it's not easy to express gratitude when life sucks, but it is possible and very, very necessary. We may just need to look a little harder.

AWARE: Have you been neglecting to say thank you for all that you already have? Can you bring into your awareness right now at least three things you're grateful for? Have you noticed how people with an attitude of gratitude have an amazing, uplifting energy around them? Would you like to be one of those people?

ADJUST: Can you see how easily you can adjust your daily routine to bring in some moments of gratitude? Can you adjust your mindset to focus on the good in your life, rather than the negatives? Remember to go easy on yourself here if you are in a bad place at the moment, as this will take some considerable effort, but I can assure you, it is possible. And can you think of ways to express gratitude to others, or show more acts of kindness?

ATTRACT: Get into the habit of practising daily gratitude, from the heart, and there will be no end to the miracles you can attract into your life.

THE FREEDOM OF FORGIVENESS

Another practice to get into the habit of is forgiveness. It's right up there with gratitude in the eyes of the Universe if you want to step into your power and manifest your desires. If you're someone who finds it extremely difficult to forgive, and please understand that this includes forgiving yourself just as much as anyone else you perceive to have 'wronged' you, you'll forever remain in a victim state, feeling stuck and enduring no end of grief, turmoil and unrest. This is not a happy, high vibrational state. It doesn't matter how awful the thing that has happened; forgiveness is the only way to set yourself free.

If I was to ask you to think about pain from a physical perspective and what you'd do about it if you were suffering, I can almost guarantee you'd not hesitate to look for a way to relieve it. Imagine you have an abscess, due to a rotten tooth that's got infected. Even if you dread the dentist, I feel pretty confident you'd go to see one so that the abscess could be treated. Of course, the rotten tooth might need to be removed which would result in more pain, but if you believed it was the quickest way to ease your discomfort, I am absolutely sure you'd go for it. Let's face it; no one likes to be in pain.

Isn't it weird then that we rarely address emotional pain with the same logic and haste? Rather than freeing ourselves of whatever has caused us the emotional pain, through forgiveness, we are far more adept at turning our emotions inwards and agonising over what happened for days, weeks, maybe even years. Even if we vent our anger at the outset in an attempt to make ourselves feel better, if we don't then forgive whoever or whatever has caused us the pain, then we can never move past it. And as I've already mentioned, this includes forgiving ourselves where necessary, be it for reacting badly and flying off the handle in response to a certain situation, or not standing up for ourselves, or whatever. Why do we persist in torturing ourselves, stewing over something we can do absolutely nothing about since it's already happened and is in the past? All we're doing is allowing the 'wound' to fester.

To be a powerfully charged magnet of high vibration and attract the good stuff into our lives, we simply MUST let go of anything that is not of the same vibrational frequency. Resentment, anger, hurt, upset, guilt, shame, fear of being judged or feeling unworthy are all examples of low vibrational states. In fact, anything less than love, which carries the highest vibration. We are made of love, it is at our very core, and the more love we can give to ourselves and others, the more we'll connect with source energy and become a manifestation magnet.

But hang on a minute, I hear you say. It's all very well forgiving someone if they've cut you up in traffic or bad-mouthed you in front of your friends, but what if it's for something really bad, like abuse, or murder? How can you ever forgive someone for that and more to the point, why should you?

To be totally honest with you, there was a time I struggled with this. If I read about really bad events happening like a child being murdered, for example, I simply couldn't get my head around it if I learned the parents had forgiven the murderer. It just seemed so wrong, and like they were letting the murderer off the hook. But this is precisely why it is so important to understand forgiveness.

When you forgive someone, you are NOT condoning what they did and saying it was OK, and you are definitely not letting them off the hook! What you are doing is letting yourself off the hook, freeing yourself of any attachment to the situation to allow healing to occur. If you fail to forgive, on the other hand, the only person who will suffer is you. Forgiveness is about taking care of YOU.

Remember that whatever happened is in the past. No amount of resentment, self-loathing, guilt, shame or anger will change that. Holding onto past hurts and keeping negative feelings alive will only serve to keep you a prisoner to your pain.

It's not about right or wrong either. Even if someone has made you look like a complete idiot over something you know you're right over when they're the ones who have got it wrong, you have to ask yourself, is it worth all the stress of not letting it go? While you're getting all fired up over analysing what happened, even perhaps doubting yourself, do you imagine the other person is losing sleep over it? And is it any of your business anyway what they may or may not be thinking?

I'm not suggesting forgiveness is easy, and especially if someone has really got under your skin for something you know without a shadow of a doubt you're right about. But it may help you to look at it this way. Forgiveness is about owning your power, taking responsibility for your own happiness and fully understanding that your desire to feel good and ultimately raise your vibration, is SO much more important than scoring a few brownie points.

So how do we forgive? While this should come as second nature to us, years of social conditioning and bearing grudges could not make it further from the truth. But it is an essential skill to master if you want to live a happy and fulfilled life, where your dreams really do come true.

Compassion is key, as is appreciating that you may need to feel uncomfortable in the short term, to reap long-term benefit like my example with the rotten tooth. You'd rather do anything than go to the dentist, but at the same time you know it's likely to be your quickest route to a pain-free conclusion.

It may be helpful to understand that when people act poorly it's generally out of fear, pain or misunderstanding. Undoubtedly there will be times when someone acts like a complete idiot just for the sheer hell of it, but it's less typically the case. Often they won't have even realised how much they've upset you. Remember too that we have no idea what is going on in their life that may have caused them to act the way they have. Don't assume and don't judge.

Use irritating situations as an opportunity for growth, not pain, by asking yourself what you can learn from them. Again, this can be difficult to do, since the last thing you want to accept is that you've attracted an unpleasant person or situation to you. But like it or not, especially if you find a certain pattern emerging, this may well be the case. It certainly was for me.

In my early years as a nutritionist, I found it necessary to supplement my therapist income and took on part-time office work. I enjoyed administrative roles and was quite happy in an office environment, but after reaching complete burnout for the third time in succession, I had to take a long hard look in the mirror. While each of the three jobs was completely different, they also had many similarities. They'd all evolved into hugely stressful management positions, with unrealistic expectations crammed into part-time hours. The more efficient and capable I proved myself to be, the more I was given to do and the less support I received. It was like I was on a hamster wheel going round and round, faster and faster, never seeming to get anywhere, or be able to get off!

No amount of blaming my boss, the workload, or my job-share colleagues made me feel any better or made my life easier. I was utterly miserable, and family life began to suffer as a consequence. I was completely stuck in victim mentality. Life just wasn't fair. Why did this keep happening 'to' me?

It was only after I took that look in the mirror and was completely honest with myself, that it became crystal clear. There was no mistake about it; each of my previous job roles revealed a common thread. While it wasn't pleasant to admit, the common denominator each time was me. I had allowed each of the situations to unfold and then reacted badly when they had, and I'd felt trapped and backed into a corner. I had to learn to say NO when necessary, to resist the temptation to be a perfectionist and to ask for help and equally importantly accept it when the going got tough. And I absolutely needed to practise forgiveness.

If you want to live your best life, don't look for revenge, justice, or even an apology from whoever you think may have wronged you, just move on. The longer you stew over what's happened, the worse you'll feel and will continue to feel, believe me. And you'll just keep attracting more of the same, so it really isn't worth it. It's also important to be mindful of who you look up to and spend the majority of your time with. Make a conscious effort to hang out with positive, happy people!

Take a moment to think about what's getting you down at the moment, or who you may need to forgive and remember, this could very well be you. If you have a tendency to be especially hard on yourself, like I've been in the past, then I'd encourage you to start with some self-love. If you typically react from a place of fear, then understand this is ego-based and can have immense repercussions. Don't give into or dwell on these feelings, as they will lower your vibration.

True forgiveness is not like sticking a plaster on a wound. It's important to be genuine and to forgive at a deep level. If you neglect to do this properly, you'll only receive temporary relief, before the same person or situation niggles you again. Say for example; there's one particular person who is really annoying you at the moment. Instead of incessantly bitching about them to anyone who will listen, you first need to ask yourself if they could be mirroring something in you that you need to work on changing? Oh yes, you heard me correctly! This can be uncomfortable to admit to and certainly not fun, but it may well be the reason this person or situation keeps showing up for you. Remember, you may have a lesson to be learned. If you struggle with this, ask the Universe to help you.

While it's important you try to understand the person and why they acted the way they did, it is also essential you fully appreciate it's NOT a reflection on you, but of their own fears and ego. If someone is controlling for example, then it may be because they are fearful of losing control. These people need love and understanding, not judgement, anger, or resentment. Imagine stepping into their shoes and do your absolute utmost to understand what's going on for them.

If you still feel the need to vent your frustration, then find a way that doesn't involve bitching and backstabbing. I was heavily involved in karate when I was going through some of my particularly challenging years, and there was nothing like punching and kicking a bag or full-on sparring to release pent up emotions! You can scream if that's your thing, but I'd probably suggest you do this somewhere private, or it may look like you've totally lost the plot. Just saying…

Another great option is to write a letter. It should be one of forgiveness and also gratitude. Thank the person for showing you how you don't want to be and for their part in helping you learn the lessons you need to learn. The intention here is to get your emotions out and show the Universe that you're really sincere about forgiveness. It's not about giving the person the letter. Some people find the ritual of burning it once it's finished is very liberating. But whatever you choose to do, understand that it can be a very powerful way of helping you forgive on a deep and meaningful level.

When you master the skill of forgiveness and genuinely let go of all the crap over how people have 'made' you think or feel, this will have a MASSIVE positive effect and will really help to set you free. Don't forget, it's what you focus on you'll end up manifesting more of, so let go of all the stories that are keeping you trapped, move on and be happy. Remember, forgiveness is not about letting someone off the hook; it's about owning your power and taking care of YOU.

> "It's my view that we create a life of abundance when we remember we're one with God, when we've chosen to forgive and when we see that we deserve miracles because we are a miracle."
>
> — KYLE GRAY, ANGEL PRAYERS

AWARE: Are you aware of any negative experiences that keep repeating themselves? Can you bring into your awareness now anyone who really gets under your skin? Can you identify any lessons you may be required to learn? Are you being too hard on yourself over something and hanging onto emotional pain?

ADJUST: Are there any adjustments you can commit to NOW, to forgive someone (or yourself), to set yourself free? Can you adjust your mindset to view negative repetitive patterns as a shout out from the Universe that there's a lesson you need to learn? Can you take the action steps necessary to sincerely forgive? Remember this can be as simple as writing a letter and then burning it, by way of a gesture to the Universe that you're ready to release. And don't forget to ask the Universe to help you, especially if you find this particularly difficult to do.

ATTRACT: Master the art of forgiveness, and you will surely attract manifestation and miracles into your life.

MEDITATION & MASTERY

I mentioned in Part 1 the importance of being present and how it's actually the only moment in time we have any actual control over. But how can we practise this in our day to day life? After all, it's so easy to worry about things in the past, to overanalyse how we could have done things differently, or equally to get caught up with anxieties about the future. And this couldn't be more clearly demonstrated now, as I find myself writing this chapter in the grip of a viral pandemic. Never before have I experienced such a global challenge, with the entire UK being one of many countries currently in total lockdown.

Scaremongering headlines dominate the news, and no one can escape the negative posts across all social media platforms either. While the intention may well be to keep us updated of important developments, the negatively biased reporting does not benefit anyone. In fact, as more and more people plunge into the depths of fear, it only serves to lower the vibration of mass consciousness as a whole. Aside from the damage this does to our mental health, ironically, it also lowers our immune resistance at a time we need it to be especially strong.

I'm not going to pretend I have no concerns at the moment and am living in a total zen-like state. My husband has only just finished the chemotherapy for his cancer and as such his immunity is likely to be very low, meaning he falls into a high-risk category, not only for contracting this current virus but of potentially facing a worst-case scenario if he did. It would be irresponsible and foolish of me not to take the threat seriously. But I refuse to let it dominate my thoughts and be overwhelmed by all the what-ifs. The futility of this was highlighted to me during his cancer journey, as I've already told you. Stressing over circumstances beyond our control only serves to rob us of any peace of mind and of precious moments we can share with all those we love NOW. None of us can predict with any level of certainty how future events will pan out, so we really need to stop wasting so much valuable time there, and meditation really can help with this.

So what's all the fuss about; what is meditation? It actually dates back to Hinduism and forms an integral part of the Buddhist religion, although it's been practised in one form or another across virtually every religion in recorded history. Not that it is in itself a religion, nor do you need any religious beliefs to practise it, or reap the benefits. It's more widely accepted as a spiritual practice, although if we're going to get really finickity, it's perhaps more accurately described as a science. This is because it's based upon a set of specific principles that produce verifiable results. But don't get caught up on all of this. Meditation is simply the best way to collect our thoughts, jump off the hamster wheel of life and reach that position of inner peace and BEING.

While it's a wonderfully simple practice, it can be inherently difficult for many to master. The aim is to remain fully awake while allowing the mind to settle to one of stillness, although this in itself takes some perseverance. In fact, it's typically the mind that offers the most resistance and is the biggest obstacle preventing us from reaching this awareness. Don't let this put you off though, as the rewards will be worth it and, at the end of the day, we're not looking for perfection here.

Of course, you may already be saying it's not for you. Perhaps you've tried meditating in the past and are one of those people with a mind that point-blank refuses to quieten. Sound familiar? Please take heart if so, as you're most definitely not alone. In fact, let me share a little secret with you... I'm like that too! But it may surprise you to learn that we're not actively trying to quieten the mind, as it's futile to even try. The more you use conscious effort to force your mind into stillness, the busier it will become.

What you're actually aiming for is to let it settle of its own accord, at least for brief moments during your meditation practice. Just be consistent and surrender to the process.

One of my previous office-based roles was working for a charitable organisation delivering courses for transcendental meditation, TM. I hadn't long lost my dad to cancer when I took on the position, and I was also learning to cope with my mum's early-stage dementia. You could say it was a pretty stressful time! I remember meditating religiously, desperately hoping that by doing so I'd find some inner peace and guidance. Much to my frustration, however, what I actually experienced was incessant mind chatter that nearly drove me mad! I decided I had to be doing something wrong. Maybe I was trying too hard? Or not hard enough? I told myself meditation obviously didn't work for me. But I knew from my conversations with some of the TM teachers at the time and indeed with people who had taken the courses, that it did have very real benefits for the mind, body and spirit. And I definitely wanted some of that.

One day I spoke with the founder of the charity about my disappointing meditation practice and what I'd been experiencing. What he told me not only made me feel a whole lot better at the time, but it has always stuck in my mind. All he said was that we should never judge a meditation by the meditation itself, but what happens outside of it. If you find your mind is really busy during meditation, then it's a sure sign your body is releasing stress, which of course is a good thing. It doesn't mean you'll not notice benefits over time, regardless of how frantic your meditations may remain. You may suddenly realise your anxiety has improved, or that you're coping more calmly and objectively with stress. Or you may find you become more productive during your working day, another common benefit, which is quite ironic when you consider how many people say they don't have the time to meditate!

Some of the other scientifically-proven benefits of meditation that may become part of your experience include:

- Lower blood pressure
- Improved blood circulation
- Lower heart rate
- Slower respiratory rate
- Reduced stress and anxiety
- Lower blood cortisol levels
- Improved feelings of wellbeing
- Deeper relaxation

So I guess what I'm saying is that whatever your experience of meditation might be, don't get frustrated, compare your experience to someone else's, or make any judgement at all. Just allow it to happen. I can assure you that your experience will be just as it's meant to be at that moment. All you're basically doing is giving yourself permission to recharge your batteries, rather like enjoying a mini-retreat! The technique serves to bring about a state of consciousness that is different from your normal waking state and enables you to go within and experience your true inner being and centre of consciousness. Yogi's refer to this as our state of bliss.

Another thing not to get caught up on is how to meditate. Many techniques exist, and you may well be told one is superior to another, but to my mind, there is no right or wrong. Just find what works for you. In general, the easiest way to begin meditating is by focusing on the breath. Alternatively, you can repeat a single word or mantra, stare at a candle flame, or listen to a repetitive gong.

Mindfulness is another option, and the possibilities with this technique are limitless! You can practise mindfulness when you're out walking, or taking some other form of exercise, or even as you're doing the housework or washing up. It just involves giving all your attention to the task or activity at the time. If you're out walking, for example, you would bring your awareness to every step, the sound of your footsteps and texture of the ground, the wind on your face, your breathing, the sights and smells around you; every little detail. It just helps to ensure you are entirely present in the moment. But let's get back to meditation...

While meditation requires no effort, I am well aware it can still appear challenging at first. I've therefore included an example meditation below, suitable for a beginner. Alternatively, if you don't feel ready to be left to your own devices, check out the hundreds of meditations on YouTube. You may prefer a guided meditation at first, or want to enjoy some soft music playing in the background. Or you may choose to meditate in complete silence, as with the practice of TM. Remember there is no right or wrong so just find what works for you, but be consistent. Start by meditating for just a few minutes initially and work up to longer durations, as and when you feel ready. Five minutes daily is far better for you overall than a one-hour meditation once a week.

The following is an example of a simple meditation:

- Begin by sitting comfortably on the floor with your legs crossed, or on a chair is equally fine, but ideally, ensure your back is straight. You can lay down, but the risk then is that you'll fall asleep, so it's not ideal. Having said that, please don't worry if you do fall asleep during meditation, as this is an indication that your body needs the extra rest.
- Close your eyes and bring your awareness to your body. Note any areas of tension and work through them, allowing your muscles to relax.
- Once your body is relaxed, focus your attention on the breath. Make no effort to control it; simply breathe naturally. Notice whether you are breathing from your diaphragm, (belly breathing) which is what you're after, or from your chest. But again, observe without judgement.
- Continue to focus your attention on your breath,

without controlling its pace or intensity. Your mind will almost certainly wander, but as soon as you become aware of those thoughts, just acknowledge them without judgement or reaction. Bear in mind that it's not the thought itself that can disturb you, but your reaction to it. Just release the thoughts as you become aware of them and return your focus back to your breath.

- Maintain this meditation practice for just a few minutes to begin with, and then gradually increase it to a longer duration once you feel comfortable.

AWARE: Are you aware you're letting stress get the better or you? Is your mind always buzzing? Are you finding it difficult to sleep at night, or focus during the day? Are you facing particular challenges at the moment? Are you aware of wasting time mulling over past events or circumstances, or worrying about future events?

ADJUST: I've explained how meditation need not take long, so can you commit to making the necessary adjustments to fit it into your day? Remember that if you're currently telling yourself that you don't have time, this is merely an excuse and one that is not serving you. Regular meditators are found to be more focused and productive, so imagine the time you could potentially clawback if it became a habit of yours and you end up being way more efficient! Carve out some time, set it in stone and make it non-negotiable.

ALLOW: Don't worry about your meditation experience; just surrender to the Universe and go with the flow. Meditation is the perfect time to connect to all that is and benefit from divine guidance and wisdom. Set an intention before you meditate, or ask questions or for any guidance you may need at the time. And then be prepared to listen and to ALLOW!

AWESOME AFFIRMATIONS

I was introduced to the power of affirmations by the amazing Louise Hay, after reading her book 'You Can Heal Your Life'. It was one of the first books I read on the subject of personal and spiritual development, and I found it wonderfully refreshing. Despite making me painfully aware of the extent of the negative self-talk I fed myself every day, it gave me hope that there was, in fact, a very simple solution to it. And affirmations are simple. We use them every day without even realising it, although sadly more so in a negative way and so therefore, not in our favour.

So what are affirmations? Basically, anything and everything we repeatedly say to ourself is an affirmation, good or bad. When we affirm something to be true regardless of whether or not it is, it's like sowing a seed in a garden. If we repeatedly tell ourselves the same thing, whether in our mind or out loud, it's like watering that seed every day, and it will grow. But here's the thing. If you want to grow sunflowers, you have to plant sunflower seeds. You can't expect to plant tulip seeds and grow sunflowers! Common sense yes, and yet so many of us are trying to do just that.

Remember, affirmations are what we repeatedly tell ourselves. If this happens to be that we're fat or stupid, or that we always end up in an abusive relationship, or whatever it is we're persistently focusing on, then these are what seeds we are planting. They will become part of our identity and show up in our reality. Of course, the trick then is to focus on positive affirmations. We need to catch ourselves in the act of saying or thinking something negative, as this will still happen, and replace it with a positive affirmation instead.

Our subconscious mind has the mammoth task of processing somewhere in the region of 40 million bits of information a second. Thankfully for our sanity, it filters this information right back to as little as five bits per second, so as not to completely overwhelm us. And it's from these five or so pieces of information that we perceive our reality, which isn't very much when you think about it. Our conscious mind works at this surface level and is the logical, analytical part of us, whereas our subconscious mind is our deepest self.

> "Imagine you are a lake. The surface of the lake changes according to weather, wind, rain etc, but the depth of the lake always remains undisturbed. The depth of the lake is your inner state, not dependent on external things."
>
> — ECKHART TOLLE

Stating affirmations in the present.

Since our subconscious mind cannot differentiate between right or wrong, past or future, it is fundamentally important to state affirmations in the positive and as already being true, regardless of whether or not this is the case. If you're currently overweight for example, it may be because you've kept on telling yourself you're fat (negative affirmation). However, it's not good enough to say you don't want to be fat, as you're still focusing on being fat and this is what the Universe and your subconscious will hear and think you want more of.

By merely changing it to 'I want to be slim' isn't specific enough either for your subconscious to respond, or to know exactly when you'd like this to happen. But you only have to tweak it ever so slightly to have it make all the difference. If you choose to say something like; 'I AM slim and happy' you are stating a positive affirmation in the present tense, and it's like sending a command to the Universe and your subconscious mind to make it happen. This is what you're after.

Take a moment to identify some of your negative self-talk. Can you now form some positive affirmations from them, as I did in the example above? Sometimes it's easier to do it this way around as when we know what we don't want, it's often easier to realise what we do. Take a look at some more examples below, with the last affirmation of each being the preferred choice:

I'm not intelligent enough - I don't want to be stupid - I AM intelligent enough.

I'm miserable - I don't want to be miserable - I AM happy.

I have no money - I don't want to be broke - I AM abundant, and money flows to me now.

One of Louise Hay's favourite affirmations was simply, 'I love and accept myself'.

When you start with the statement 'I Am …' you are essentially saying it's true for you right now. Even though this may not be the case as I've already mentioned, it's not about faking it until you make it, but about creating a new belief in your subconscious mind that will then do everything in its power to bring it to you.

If you struggle with affirmations and this is especially typical in the early days, it could be for several reasons.

Your affirmations must be believable to you and within your control. If there is very little possibility of the end result being achievable, however hard you will it to happen, this will obviously cause resistance. Say, for example, your affirmation is 'I AM queen of England'. I hate to break it to you, but no matter how often you repeat it, it's highly unlikely to come true. While I would always encourage you to imagine your most desired outcome and not limit your possibilities, you must still remember to keep your affirmations believable and realistic.

I'll give you another example with weight, as I've had a lot of experience with resistance here. If someone is currently overweight and desperately wants to be slim but doesn't actually believe they can do it, perhaps they've already been on every single diet known to man, then they're likely to experience a lot of resistance just by repeating the affirmation 'I am slim'. If you can't relate to this directly, I urge you to take a moment and just try. Imagine you're looking in the mirror and saying 'I am slim', but the person looking back at you is anything but. What do you think your mind will be saying to you? There's every possibility it will be saying don't be ridiculous, take a look why don't you!

The difference with this example, however, is that the outcome has every possibility of being achieved. Provided the person can work through their resistance and keep going and make any other adjustments necessary of course. But if the person gives up on the idea of affirmations thinking they're a waste of time, they could also end up blaming their weight on their lack of willpower to stick to a diet and then affirm how much of a failure they are. Not conducive to feeling good about themselves or raising their vibe!

Of course, I'm not saying affirmations alone will help you reach your desired outcome, but they can be an extremely effective tool to help rewire your brain and belief system. But if resistance remains a biggie for you, you may like to try a different approach that some would say is actually better. You see even among the spiritual and mindset arenas there is debate over the best way to use affirmations. Some will argue that by saying 'I am ..' when it's not yet true actually sets us up for resistance, as our mind will instantly disagree and say 'no you're not!'. In this case, they say the best way to use affirmations is to say instead, 'I am in the process of ... reaching my target weight' or whatever it may be.

The same thinking argues that by using affirmations with 'I am' may result in the Universe being lulled into a false sense of security and the belief that you really have already achieved your desire, so you don't need its help. Whereas if you use 'I am in the process of...' allows it to flow to you. Who knows. All I can tell you is that I've used affirmations both ways and believe they are equally effective, but try them for yourself. If you've used affirmations one particular way before without success, then try changing the language and use the other approach. But do stick with them.

Many top athletes and entrepreneurs use affirmations to help them raise their game. Why? Because they work! They understand their power where self-mastery is concerned and to have our subconscious mind work for us rather than against. When I was going for my black belt in karate, I used affirmations religiously to help me overcome my fears and self-doubt. Despite thoroughly learning the syllabus and training harder than I'd ever trained before, I still struggled with the belief I could even survive an intense six-hour grading, let alone actually achieve my black belt. I was a 45-year-old woman who had only started karate five years earlier for goodness sake! But I knew how crucial it was for me to work as hard on my mindset and beliefs, as I did on my physical fitness. I am convinced affirmations played a big part in my successful grading, as well as visualisation, but I'll cover that later.

Learning to use affirmations effectively is a skill to be mastered, just like any other skill in life. And if you continue to have negative thoughts, as you will, just acknowledge them. Awareness is empowering in itself, remember. Try using the 'cancel, clear, delete' every time a negative thought pops into your head and see if this works for you, and then throw in a positive affirmation! Get into the habit of writing down affirmations for anything you want to work on, or voice record some onto your phone. Or you can download an App onto your phone and have this not only keep a note of your affirmations but also prompt you to look at them regularly.

I am always using affirmations. I'll pin them to my notice board, on the fridge, or wherever else I'm likely to see them regularly. If I need a confidence boost for when I'm about to do something out of my comfort zone my affirmation may simply say 'I CAN do this!', or it may be more specific when I want to manifest a particular desire. Some people like to stick post-it notes all over the place, including on their mirror for affirmations like, 'I am good enough' or Louise's favourite 'I love and accept myself'. Whatever affirmations you choose to use, make them positive and personal to you, but also be sure to have fun with them too!

AWARE: Are you aware of what you repeatedly tell yourself? Is it mainly positive, or is there way too much negative self-talk going on? Are you aware now of the power of your words? Has this chapter made you think about the countless ways you could tap into the power of affirmations?

ADJUST: If there are adjustments you need to make in your life, can you now see how affirmations can help? Can you adjust the language you use, particularly to yourself and make it more positive? Can you commit to saying affirmations everyday? Remember to make them personal, positive and believable and write/say them in the present tense.

<u>ATTRACT</u>: Since affirmations help rewire our belief systems by enabling us to make new neural connections in the brain, be careful what you wish for! Remember they can be used negatively to keep you stuck, or positively to empower you and help you reach your fullest potential. Positive affirmations will help you believe in yourself and your abilities and raise your vibration. So what are you waiting for? Start using them and attract miracles!

TAP TO RELEASE & THETAHEALING®

There are countless tools at your disposal to help you release old limiting beliefs and negative thought patterns, and I now want to introduce you to another couple of my favourites, each very powerful in their own right.

Emotional Freedom Technique

Emotional Freedom Technique (EFT), also commonly referred to as tapping, is credited to have many beneficial effects. And the beauty with tapping is that the results can be noticed almost instantaneously, depending on the severity of the issue and what you want to achieve.

Nick Ortner, author of 'The Tapping Solution', explains it like this. "Tapping is a powerful holistic healing technique that has been proven to effectively resolve a range of issues, including stress, anxiety, phobias, emotional disorders, chronic pain, addiction, weight control, and limiting beliefs, just to name a few."

The originator of EFT, Gary Craig, based the technique on modern psychology in combination with acupressure, an ancient Chinese healing discipline. It helps to calm the nervous system and restore the balance of lifeforce energy and also has the ability to actually rewire the brain to respond in a more positive and healthier way. During a tapping session, you simply tap on specific points of the body using your fingertips, while focusing on negative emotions or any physical issue or pain you may be experiencing.

It's not merely random tapping, however, as the points used directly correspond to meridian endpoints, which are like energy superhighways throughout your body. The meridians connect every organ, cell, atom and all that's physical in the body, along with your emotions and spirit. Everything conscious and unconscious. But unlike with acupressure and acupuncture where you'd have to learn the specific points in relation to the organ or pathway it supports, the beauty with EFT is that you don't need to know.

Interestingly at first glance, EFT seems almost to be in direct contradiction to how affirmations are used, which led to some resistance on my part to this technique initially. Affirmations focus very much on making positive statements in the present tense, as you now know, while EFT works differently. It is typical of this technique to start with a negative 'setup' statement. I know, crazy right, but there is a reason for it.

Let me give you an example to help explain further. Before you begin any actual tapping, you are encouraged to tune into your body to assess how a particular negative thought, belief or emotion is making you feel, on a scale of one to ten typically. This helps provide a point of reference for instant feedback following each round of tapping. A round is completed once you have tapped on each point following a set sequence. The tapping points include the top of the head, the eyebrow, side of the eye, underneath the eye, under the nose, the chin, the collarbone and under the arm.

Let's say you are in physical pain. Initially, you'd assess the extent of your pain on the scale of one to ten, and for argument's sake, we'll rate it at a ten. Your setup statement could be; 'Even though I have all this pain in my body ...' Or better still, be as specific as you can and say exactly where the pain is; 'Even though I have this excruciating pain in my knee ...'

What you're doing here is acknowledging the pain, but in a completely non-judgemental way and to 'prove' it, you finish by saying; '... I deeply and completely love and accept myself'. Your full setup statement is, therefore; 'Even though I have this excruciating pain in my knee, I deeply and completely love and accept myself'.

The statement is repeated three times, during which you tap on what is called the karate chop point on the side of the hand, below your little finger. You then follow the generally recognised sequence of tapping points I mentioned earlier, saying only part of the setup statement, for example, 'this pain in my knee'. It is quite typical to start with negative statements but work on releasing them and then affirm more positive ones as you work through the round or each subsequent round. For the setup statement I've used the subsequent statements could be; 'this pain in my knee'; 'it's really hurting me'; 'it's getting me down'; 'I choose to release it now'; 'releasing this pain in my knee'; 'feeling totally pain-free now'. So you see how it evolves into a positive statement.

One round may be all you need to notice an improvement or it may be necessary to do several rounds over a number of days. You determine your level of improvement by tuning back into your body as you did in the beginning and reassessing your score. Pain typically responds quite quickly and so after just a single round of tapping your score may go down quite noticeably. In my example, that initial score of ten may now have reduced to a score of eight or lower. The idea is to continue the rounds until the score reduces to some level of significance.

If you are interested to learn more about the science and history behind tapping, the sequence of tapping points, and how to get started, please check out the resource section at the back of the book. I have included the link to Nick Ortner's website, The Tapping Solution, where you'll find various free resources.

I'm also a huge fan of Brad Yates, and you can follow along with any one of his hundreds of tapping sequences on YouTube and subscribe to his channel. I don't think it's possible there's a topic he hasn't covered! If nothing else this will help to familiarise yourself with the tapping points and have you understand the wording to use as you work through them, although I've come to realise there is no right or wrong with these as they are personal to you.

I may have made it sound complicated, but it really isn't, and you can master the technique in no time. But going back to the negative setup, you may still be wondering why this is necessary, as I did when I first came across this technique. As I mentioned, I struggled with tapping in the early days because of it. Louise Hay had been one of my most influential personal growth 'gurus', and she was all for positive affirmations and self-love. This had really resonated with me whereas, before I had a better understanding of tapping, this seemed to be reinforcing negatives. I seriously didn't need to be doing that!

But now I understand the reason for this negative start point, it totally makes sense. It enables you to clear out the old and make way for the new. If you have a lot of limiting beliefs, are suffering in pain, or whatever it may be, you'll be holding onto a lot of negative energy. By acknowledging it without judgement, you can then work on clearing and releasing it.

Funnily enough, it turned out that Louise Hay was herself a great fan of tapping. And not only that but she was actually interviewed by Nick Ortner at one of his events and asked her response to the whole negative setup question. Her reply was simple. If you want to clean your house, you first have to take out the trash! Genius.

So I really encourage you to check out EFT if you haven't already and add it to your personal and spiritual growth toolkit. There are so many ways you can reap the benefits of this simple but effective technique, and it can easily be learned and incorporated as part of your regular routine.

ThetaHealing®

ThetaHealing® is something I've come across much more recently. It's a world-renowned healing method that was created by Vianna Stibal in 1995 during her recovery from cancer and her personal journey back to health. Put very simply, it combines meditation with spiritual philosophy but is not specific to any religion. The purpose of Theta is to get closer to the Creator, and as such, it is a powerful healing modality. On her website Vianna explains, "It is a training method for your mind, body and spirit that allows you to clear limiting beliefs and live life with positive thoughts, developing virtues in all that you do. Through meditation and prayer, the ThetaHealing® Technique creates a positive lifestyle."

Despite being new to this healing discipline, I have already witnessed its power and potential, especially for releasing limiting beliefs, which is why I felt it was worth bringing to your attention. But my journey has literally only just begun, and so I'll not go into it any further here. Vianna has written numerous books on the subject, each building on the one before, so if you are interested in learning more, this would be a great place to start. I have also included a link to her website in the resource section at the end of the book.

EXCEPTIONAL ESSENTIAL OILS

Limiting beliefs aside, if you're looking to take your vibration to the next level, then there's no better way than by harnessing the exceptional power of pure essential oils like lavender and frankincense. Like Mother Nature's steroids, scientific studies have shown that essential oils vibrate at a higher frequency than any other substance known to man. And just by smelling, diffusing, or topically applying a therapeutic grade essential oil, you can raise your vibration almost immediately!

Not only will this enhance your spiritual connection, wellbeing and joy, but essential oils are also reported to improve mental concentration and support you on a physical level too. They create a hostile environment for pathogens like bacteria and viruses and support the efficient functioning of the immune system generally. They can also be used to clear negative energy in your environment and raise the vibration of anyone within it. They truly are the most amazing gifts Mother Nature has given us, which is why I have no hesitation using them in my business.

So what's the secret behind their unparalleled power? If you take into account our sense of smell is instant, the most powerful of all our senses BY FAR, and has the strongest link to our subconscious mind and emotions, it's pretty self-explanatory. The reason for their effectiveness is right there, plain and simple. All I can say is, if you don't already use them, I highly encourage you to start!

But a word of caution here; you must choose wisely. You get what you pay for, whether it's a nutritional or herbal health supplement or essential oil. Many cheaper brands are synthetic, chemically processed and highly diluted, and are often stored incorrectly, which means they're as good as useless with significantly lower vibration. It is absolutely imperative you choose 100% pure, certified grade essential oils. It's also worth noting that the most potent oils will have been sourced from the country they are indigenous to.

Pure essential oils that have been carefully extracted are living substances and have a high vibration, but the actual frequency varies according to the oil. Rose, lavender, jasmine and frankincense are some of the highest vibration oils, making them the most powerful. To help put this into perspective, the 'average' healthy human body resonates at a frequency between 62-72 MHz (megahertz), while pure essential oils can vary anywhere from 52 MHz to a whopping 320 MHz! The frequencies of some common essential oils are:

- Rose 320 MHz
- Frankincense: 147 MHz
- Lavender: 118 MHz
- Sandalwood: 98 MHz
- Peppermint: 78 MHz
- Basil: 52 MHz

Pure essential oils can raise your frequency in as little as 22 seconds! And if you really want to maximise their benefits for your highest potential, there's no better way than combining them with a positive mindset, prayer and intent. Not only will they raise your vibration and benefit your wellbeing in so many ways, but essential oils also smell divine and can be used as a safe alternative to perfume (many of which contain toxic chemicals).

The simplest way to use essential oils is by inhaling. Simply add a drop of the oil onto your palms, gently rub them together and then cup them over your nose and take a few slow, deep breaths. Sorted! Of course, you can also diffuse essential oils, apply them topically (with caution as some may need to be combined with a carrier oil), or enjoy them as part of a wonderful aromatherapy massage. Some may even be added to food but again, with caution, as not all are suitable for this.

For more information on essential oils and guidance towards a premium quality range, please check out the resource section at the end of the book.

ASK YOUR ANGELS

I've already introduced you to some fantastic tools that you can implement straight away, to begin creating positive changes in your life. It's all about showing up, owning your space and taking responsibility for where you are and ultimately, for where you're going too. But there's one major subject I've not mentioned, and yet it's fundamental in my opinion for our spiritual growth, happiness and wellbeing. It doesn't matter where you are right now, whether you're in a positive, happy place or overwhelmed and stuck, it's so important to remember you are never alone; the Universe really does have your back. Always. Now I suspect I already know the answer to this since you're reading this book, but I'm going to ask you anyway. Do you believe in angels?

I'm not asking if you've seen them, felt their presence or had any magical experience. I just want to know if you believe? Some people question whether they're real, particularly if they have no religious beliefs, or worry that if they don't have clairvoyant abilities and can't see their angels, they won't be able to connect with them. This simply isn't true. Angels are not only very real, but they're with each and every one of us always, regardless of our religious beliefs or otherwise. Indeed, angels transcend religion. We all have access to them without exception and can call upon them for guidance and support just as often as we choose. But this is the key. Angels honour our free will and so will not intervene and help us unless we ask. They're actually not allowed to, due to the law of free will, except under extreme circumstances. But once we make the connection, there is no limit to how they can help enrich our lives.

Kyle Gray, an international speaker, bestselling author and renowned authority on angels, describes them beautifully. "An angel is pure, sacred energy," he says. "They are the heartbeat of the universe or a brainwave of the Divine, focused on your wellbeing."

Angels are spiritual beings of light from the higher dimensions. In accordance with divine will, their purpose is to serve us as we navigate our earthly journey, with their ultimate desire being to help us live our best, happiest and most fulfilled life. They want us to laugh and have fun, they want us to nurture great relationships, and they want us to be the epitome of love. Our angels comfort us when we're feeling low, show us the way when we are lost, and provide a gentle nudge and extra guidance to help us fulfil our life's purpose. There is no end to the ways they can support us, whether our issue is emotional, physical or spiritual, or we're just looking for some extra help to manifest positive experiences into our life. They can actually change the vibrational energy field around us. Provided the request we make is for our highest good and that of others, our angels will help us every step of the way with their own divine inspiration.

From a spiritual perspective, I like to think of angels as being heavenly messengers, who act to deepen our understanding and connection to the Creator and open lines of communication. Whenever we ask our angels to help us, we connect to the love and power of the Creator and invite divine will to guide us, rather than struggling to push on ahead under our own steam. Remember that the feeling of being overwhelmed and losing control is almost certainly the work of the ego and will always be hard work. Rather like wading through treacle! So doesn't it make sense to open up instead, and connect to the immense support network of the Universe that is available to us?

If you're familiar with the angelic realm, then you'll already know there is quite a hierarchy among them. And as I've said, they are all ready and willing to serve us whenever we invite them to do so. Healing angels, peace angels and archangels are just a few examples, but there are far too many to mention for the purposes of this book. I'd not be able to do them anywhere near the justice they deserve! But if your knowledge of angels is limited, I would encourage you to research them further, or you'll risk missing out on the best support system available to you.

Having said that, I would like to give a special mention to your very own guardian angel. Assigned to you before you were even born, your guardian angel has made a sacred vow to protect and guide you throughout your entire life. They are pure, unconditional love and regardless of what you do, are never judgemental and will never leave you. As far as they are concerned, you are a perfect creation of the Divine, and they always want the best for you. Think of your guardian angel like your best friend, who wants nothing more than to be an integral part of your life. They delight in celebrating your wins just as much as they'll support you whenever you need it.

Connecting with your Angels

But how do you actually connect with them? Some people neglect to call upon their angels because they're not sure how to go about it and overcomplicate things. Yes, you can speak to them by way of formal prayer, but you can just as easily chat to them as you would a close friend. The more you get into the habit of asking your angels for help, the more they'll be able to assist you. And the more you raise your vibration by tuning into them, the more open you'll become to their clear divine guidance and healing frequency.

Angels are high vibrational spiritual beings, and in order to tune into their energy, you'll ideally want to be in a relaxed, meditative state. Before I go into meditation, I always ask my angels to reveal to me what I need to know and quite often I'll ask them again as I go to sleep. And if I have a burning question I'd like an answer to, then I'll ask that specifically. I may not get an answer straight away, but something usually happens over the course of the next few days to help me with this. When I don't have a specific question to ask, I simply say, 'how may I best serve'?

Prayer is another powerful way to connect and provides the opportunity to ask for guidance or answers to specific questions. But you must be prepared to listen for the answers you seek and notice signs too. As I've already said, answers are not always given in the way we might expect. They may come through by way of a song that plays on the radio, a feather in a place you'd not expect to see one, or multiple number sequences that keep repeating. These are all ways our angels try to connect with us.

Showing gratitude in our prayers is another tip Kyle Gray shares, and he says it makes them especially powerful. He recommends that instead of saying 'please angels can you help me with …' we are better to say, 'thank you, angels, for …' Not only are we expressing our gratitude, but also our faith they will get the job done like it's a foregone conclusion. "A prayer is that moment when we allow the Universe to support our endeavours," says Kyle. We must be in no doubt at all that they will help us and another way to do this is by finishing our prayer by saying 'and so it is', or 'it is done'.

Visualisation is another tool you can use to connect with your angels. You can visualise them directly, or see yourself immersed in warm, golden light, rather like being wrapped in a comforting blanket. But don't worry if you're not able to 'see' them in the true sense of the word. Visualisation is another skill that needs some time and practice to master, and even then, you may never see them. But this doesn't mean you won't come to feel their presence, or just have a gentle knowing that they are with you.

While I've talked about meditation and prayer, it's not always possible, of course, to connect with your angels in this calm, relaxed way. This is particularly the case if you're very suddenly faced with a traumatic, dangerous or even life-threatening situation. But there have been numerous accounts of where angels have stepped in to help people at such times when the request for their intervention was instant. This is also one of the very few occasions where angels may be allowed to help us, even if we don't, or can't ask. So whether you have time to meditate or not, please rest assured your angels will step in when you need them!

Get into the habit of connecting with your angels. Thank them in advance for their help and guidance, and trust whatever comes to you. They want to be a part of your life, so open up and let them in!

AWARE: Are you aware of angels? Have certain things or events happened that have made you wonder if they're around you? Have you ever noticed a feather appear in a place you'd not expect to see one, or multiple number sequences? Your angels may well be trying to connect with you...

ADJUST: If you've neglected to welcome angels into your life before now, do you understand why this will not be serving you? And how easy it is to call upon them? Can you open up your heart and let them in?

ATTRACT: Tap into this wonderful support system by calling upon your angels for guidance and support, and they truly will enrich your life. Your gift from the Creator to help you attract all the love and abundance your heart desires.

PART 3 - ATTRACTING ABUNDANCE

MANIFESTING - A MATTER OF VIBRATION

OK, so the big question is; can we follow a spiritual path and yet still want to manifest certain things in our life? We are taught to be grateful for what we have and to live in the present, so does that mean we shouldn't have aspirations to want or achieve certain things? Does it make us a bad person to want more? Of course not. The Universe wants for us to have the best life experience possible, just like our angels, and this includes limitless abundance. The only really important thing NOT to get caught up thinking is that it'll take what we want to have or achieve, in order for us to be happy, or that the 'thing' will define us. This is not true. Constantly looking for external sources for happiness, or validation from others is the work of our misguided ego. True happiness is an inside job.

Countless books have been written about the Law of Attraction, 'The Secret' by Rhonda Byrne being a classic example and another favourite of mine, 'Ask and It Is Given' by Esther and Jerry Hicks. Having dreams and setting goals not only improves our motivation and encourages us to focus, but they also help to raise our vibration to match the frequency or energy of what we're looking to attract. And as you well know by now, this is the key. It's rather like tuning into a radio station; our energy must match that of what we're trying to bring into our reality. As I've said before, if we're in a high vibrational state, we are far more likely to manifest our desires, whereas if we're constantly vibrating at a low level, the opposite will be true. Let me explain this in more detail now.

If you focus entirely on lack, or what you don't want, the Universe will misinterpret your signals and give you more of the same. Energy goes where attention flows. If you want to lose weight for example, but concentrate solely on how much you hate being fat, the Universe will only pick up on your constant thoughts about being fat and so you'll stay fat. Similarly, if you want financial freedom but focus all the time on being broke and not having money to pay your bills or to afford the things you want, then you're actually sending out signals of lack. The very thing you want to flow into your life, money, you will be blocking by constantly focusing on not having enough. You have to remember and truly believe that there's nothing you can't do, be or have. Everything you could ever want is available to you, and the best way to keep this belief strong is by connecting to Source energy and remaining there.

> "Abundance is the experience in which all our needs are easily met, and our desires spontaneously fulfilled."
>
> — DEEPAK CHOPRA

When we're happy, healthy and vital in every moment of our existence, and feel as though we have a purpose, this is true abundance.

Fear energy in any form blocks abundance, as does low self-worth. If deep inside you don't feel as though you deserve what you've set your heart on manifesting, then it's not likely to show up for you. And it doesn't matter how much you work with the law of attraction; it will all be in vain if for some reason or another you don't allow yourself to receive. It may be that you're more comfortable giving than receiving, but both are of equal importance. Not only will you do yourself a disservice if you're always giving as you'll block your own abundance, but ultimately this will affect your capacity to pay it forwards. Let me give you an example from a monetary point of view, as this is an area I have struggled with over the years.

Coming from a therapist background and genuinely wanting to help others, I was definitely more comfortable giving than receiving. I found it almost cringe-worthy charging for my services and advice, and would often cut my fees or even give advice and therapies for free. Not only did this result in a business that was not even covering my expenses, but it also meant I was limited to who I could help. And as far as the Universe was concerned, I was shouting out loud and clear that I wasn't worthy and deserving, and that my time wasn't of value. So guess what? People took advantage of me, cancelled appointments at the last minute or just completely failed to show up. I didn't value my time, so how could I expect anyone else to?

I knew I had specific blocks around money that had stemmed from childhood. I remember constantly hearing how money didn't grow on trees or buy you happiness, and how it made people materialistic and greedy. I found this confusing as a child growing up in a household reasonably well off, with my dad being a successful chartered accountant, and it led to different issues over money as I became a teenager. When I was bullied at school, there were times I was called a snob, and I convinced myself it was because we lived in a big house. Instead of being grateful for where we lived, I chose to blame this and my parents for my unhappiness.

However, despite what money we had as a family, there were always negative feelings around it and fear of lack, especially as far as Mum was concerned. But I'd also weaved into the mix my own belief that if you had money then people would be cruel to you and I didn't want any of that. I just wanted to fit in, be kind and help people. It certainly didn't occur to me I could have both. I hadn't come across the law of attraction, or how the abundance of the Universe was ours for the taking. I just made an unconscious decision that money was not a good idea and led to all sorts of complications. Of course, not having it leads to complications of its own!

The bottom line is this; money is neither good nor bad; it's merely energy. It's the attachment and beliefs we hook onto it that determines whether we view it in a positive or negative light. And it's this that affects its vibration and gives it the power over us, one way or another. But even knowing this, it has taken me years to release my unease over money and the very mixed feelings of wanting to earn more of my own but then feeling guilty because I did. It's not like we needed more 'stuff'. My husband had always provided well for us as a family, but I dearly wanted to be able to contribute more and relieve some of the pressure from him.

Even so and despite my good intentions, it became apparent to me on reflection that I was trying to manifest from a place of unworthiness. There was the guilt for not being able to contribute more and the frustration that no matter how hard I worked, and I worked really hard, my income always seemed so insignificant. And this resulted in me feeling like a failure and even a liability at times. Now you tell me if you think I was offering up a great vibration to receive from? Plus I was still far more comfortable giving than receiving.

My lightbulb moment came one day as I was listening to Gabby Bernstein talk about abundance. She explained that if we can become unapologetic about our earning capacity, with the knowledge that our great work needs to be supported, then money will flow to us. We serve no one by playing small and denying ourselves the abundance we deserve. Think of it this way. The more money you make as a consequence of adding value and enriching the lives of others means you'll be able to help even more people in the long run. It's rather like a circle of wealth. Although I don't necessarily mean by giving it away despite that being an option, of course, and there may well be a charity close to your heart that you'd dearly like to support if finances would allow.

Perhaps you currently work a 9-5 job that doesn't inspire you in the slightest but have started your own dream business on the side that adds value to others. If you allow the money you deserve to come your way, are then able to give up the day job and focus more on the business you love, you are now able to help more people. You may even end up hiring someone else to work with you or several people! Alternatively, you could invest further in developing your life skills, perhaps take additional courses, or run events to help and support others that way. Whether you agree or not, with money comes choice. So even if you're not money-driven like me, you absolutely owe it to yourself (and others), to allow and receive. When you add value to enrich your life and the lives of those around you, the Universe will absolutely want to support you!

I hope I've managed to convince you by now that abundance is yours for the taking, but if you still have some reservations, there may be another explanation. Another very common reason why people unwittingly sabotage their manifesting ability is that they wrongly believe that by getting the things they want, it'll be at the expense of someone else. This simply isn't the case. Abundance is your natural spirit state of being and what you manifest will not deny another person. If you think about it, considering the example I gave previously, the reverse is far more accurate. Not only that, but if you raise your vibration, grow as a person and allow yourself to manifest your desires, you indirectly give permission for others to do the same. By finding your true purpose and fulfilling the mission you've been sent here to complete, you inspire others to do the same.

But a word of warning here. Don't chase after abundance, become desperate or try to force an end result. The Universe always resists force, as there's that element of doubt. It's like you're putting it out there that you're afraid it won't actually happen and this will only serve to push your desired outcome further away. No amount of throwing your heart and soul at it will change this. And at any rate, you have no way of knowing how the Universe intends to manifest what you want into your reality; it may have an even grander vision for you. So if you've already spent years trying to manifest a particular goal or dream without success, I can almost guarantee it's not because you're not good enough, worthy enough, intelligent enough, or because fate is against you. The fact of the matter is that you've found yourself trapped in a vibrational holding pattern and one that doesn't match the vibration of what you desire.

And it will be easy to spot. If you're not of a vibrational match, then you'll feel heavy and disheartened, like everything is an uphill struggle and requires so much effort. By contrast, if you're vibrating at the same frequency of your desires, you'll feel great, and the actual manifestation will simply be the icing on the cake. So pay close attention to your inner compass, as it will guide you.

Frustrating as this can be when you are out of sync, and I know from experience, there is a very fundamental solution. You have to let go of the outcome and have faith that the Universe will always lead you towards outcomes for your highest good.

My biggest realisation of this looking back, was with how I manifested my nutritional therapy course. I hadn't even come across the law of attraction back then, and I was in a bad way with postnatal depression, but even despite this, I began to develop a strong sense of purpose and a feeling of being drawn to do something. There was no doubt about the need to rebuild my self-esteem, but I also desired something I could call my own. When my husband wasn't working, he liked to spend as much time as he could get away with to go fishing. While I understood his passion and knew he deserved the break when he worked so hard, I was already struggling to cope, and so it only made things worse for me.

However, I clearly remember a conversation I had with my sister-in-law around this time. While I felt guilty just verbalising my thoughts, I confided in her about my wish to find something outside of the family for me to do. She was a beauty therapist and her own boss, which I thought was super cool, and I valued her opinion. I couldn't see me getting away with having a hobby, not with two toddlers to consider, but maybe it'd be different if I was working? We even joked about how amazing it would be if my new 'job' required me to go away on my own for a weekend every now and again like my husband went fishing.

Basically, I just put it out there to the Universe what I wanted and then let it go. I wasn't even specific on this occasion, but just imagined more how proud I would feel if I had something to call my own. It really was 'just' a dream. But not only did I manifest my nutritional therapy course, but it required me to stay up in London for a weekend once a month through the academic year! How amazing is that? And if I can achieve that without being specific, just imagine our capabilities when we hone in more precisely!

AWARE: Are you already great at manifesting, or do you find the whole process an uphill struggle? Do you feel really aligned with what you want? How do you FEEL when you think about your goals and dreams? Could you be pushing too hard? Are you aware of any blocks around manifesting abundance? Really give this some thought as remember, with awareness brings the opportunity to create positive change.

ADJUST: Have you identified any adjustments you can make to alter your point of attraction? Can you let go of the outcome and trust the Universe to deliver? Remember you're looking to connect to your inner compass, so pay attention to how you feel.

ATTRACT: Decide what you want to manifest and then let go of the outcome. Once you open up to receive and put your trust in the Universe, you can accomplish anything you want. Don't worry about connecting up all the dots; just take a step back and let the Universe lead the way.

CLEAR OUT THE TRASH

Before we move on and start looking at the actual goal-setting process, I want to lay some firm foundations to set you up for the best possible results. Of course, you may already be crystal clear on your goals and know exactly what you want and who you want to become, and if so this is AWESOME! Or you may be completely stuck... Perhaps you've found you only ever seem to get so far and then you're back where you started, or certainly not where you want to be. And this can be hugely frustrating. But wherever you find yourself now, I urge you not to skip past this chapter. While I'm not going to lie, it will be time-consuming to take action with what I'm going to present to you now, I can assure you that the potential it will have to your overall success will make it worth the effort - without any shadow of a doubt.

You see, the thing that holds many people back from truly stepping into their power and manifesting the life of their dreams is... clutter! Yes stuff, baggage, call it what you will. But if you're hanging onto a lot of emotional and energetic clutter it's like you're telling the Universe you're not quite ready to move on and still have lessons to learn. Decluttering, on the other hand, is not only very empowering, but it really shows the Universe you mean business and are ready to attract new things into your life.

So what do I actually mean by decluttering? Very simply, it means letting go of anything that no longer serves you, the 'stuff' you don't love, use, or need any more. And these are the very questions you should be asking yourself as you go about clearing the junk. When did I last use it? If it's covered in dust that should give you a pretty good clue! Do I still need it? Consider if you'd buy the same thing now if you came across it. Do I love it? Speaks for itself and if it's something that's really sentimental to you, then don't feel guilty keeping it, but make sure it's for the right reasons. After all, there's no point hanging onto something an ex gave you if they've long since moved on...

Also, ask yourself if someone else would benefit more. Remember that what you clear out doesn't necessarily need to end up in the bin. Perhaps it could be recycled, given to a friend or family member, or a charity shop. Someone else might be glad of it. But if you come across anything that's broken and can't be fixed, or you've intended to fix it for X number of years already and not got around to it, which pretty much indicates it's never likely to happen, then bin it.

If you're already shuddering at the thought as visions of that junk-filled kitchen drawer comes to mind, yes you know the one, or your wardrobe stuffed full of clothes that have not seen the light of day since you welcomed in the new millennium, I did warn you. It will take some effort, but as I've already said, the rewards will be worth it. Not only will you create a calm, peaceful and productive space, but you'll benefit from a clearer mind and sharper focus too, which brings me onto another vital aspect of the whole decluttering process. You see it's not just about clearing 'stuff', like sorting through those clothes or going through your kitchen drawers and cupboards. Getting rid of physical clutter is very important, but so is emotional decluttering and sadly, this is all too often neglected.

It is especially important if you're currently feeling overwhelmed, or fit this description more than you'd like. In fact, I'd urge you to make decluttering a priority. Honestly! Even if you're already crazy busy and are wondering how the hell you'll be able to fit it into your schedule, it's all the more reason to make sure you do. Why? Because substantial amounts of clutter in the home and/or workspace environment has been linked to overwhelm. Physical clutter leads to mental clutter and literally forces the brain to work overtime. What happens is that the mind is perpetually bombarded with excess stimulation, which is mentally exhausting. Like an ever-growing to-do list, it recognises there's always something more to be done. But if you clear the clutter, not only are you likely to feel far less over-whelmed, but it may resolve your stress completely. And it makes sense, doesn't it? When you get rid of the junk in your physical space, it allows the same to happen in your mind, which makes it far easier to think clearly, focus and prioritise.

In order to declutter thoroughly, I'd definitely recommend you consider every aspect of your life from a physical, mental and emotional perspective. I shall be giving you a few tips to help get you started, but please don't imagine I will cover everything. Your clutter will vary from someone else's, and so it's up to you to make sure you cover all that is necessary. We'll begin by tackling decluttering from a physical perspective. This includes your physical environ-ment and all the stuff in it, and also your body. So let's get started!

- Tackle small areas or simpler tasks first. If you intend to declutter your entire house (and I absolutely recommend that you do), consider one room at a time and then within that, one drawer or cupboard at a time. Don't get bogged down thinking about the enormity of the task as a whole, as this will more than likely put you off before you begin. Instead, ease yourself in gently and tackle small areas first, as you'll feel far more accomplished once you're able to start ticking them off your list. And as the energy of the space changes, which it will once you clear out the crap as decluttering is a way of dissolving and demolishing stuck and stagnant energy, this will spur you on to keep going.

- Pay particular attention to your kitchen, which in Feng Shui represents your health and wealth. Throw out broken crockery or appliances, check the expiry dates on food stored in cupboards, and don't forget your fridge and freezer.
- If you work from home and your office is currently a chaotic mess, then do something about it! Think about how much clearer your focus and productivity will be as a result. Remember, clutter creates stress.
- Transform your bedroom into a peaceful haven. There's nothing like an uncluttered bedroom to prepare you for a restful night's sleep and why not go a step further if finances will allow and treat yourself to some beautiful new bedding? At the very least, make sure it's clean and coordinated, as this will have a positive effect and make you feel special. You deserve to live in a tidy, beautiful space. And why not have a diffuser in your bedroom, to benefit from those exceptional essential oils too?

- Clear out the bathroom cabinet and again check
  expiration dates on any medication or cosmetics.
  And be sure to throw away old, threadbare towels.
  Be brutal!
- Don't neglect to clear out your handbag. Even when
  I make a conscious effort to keep mine tidy, it never
  ceases to amaze me just how quickly it attracts old
  receipts, screwed up tissues, broken pens and other
  random items.
- Pay particular attention to your purse/wallet. If
  yours is completely empty, or you have notes in
  there, but they're all screwed up and stuffed in any
  which way, what message do you think you're
  conveying to the Universe? That you don't respect
  and value money! By now you should well know
  the consequences of that...
- Bear in mind that your car is essentially an
  extension of your home, so be sure to declutter this
  too. Only keep anything you really need in it.
- You must also pay attention to your body.
  Recognise any areas that are niggling you in some
  way, whether due to any aches or pains, bloating or
  skin breakouts, right through to whether or not
  your hair needs a wash, or your nails need cutting.
  The intention here is not for you to be overly self-
  critical, but merely to raise your awareness of any
  areas of your body that may warrant some extra
  care or attention. And then indulge them!

- You'll also need to consider whether any of your relationships need decluttering. Not an easy one to tackle, but if you know in your heart of hearts there are people in your close circle who drain you with their negativity, now might be the time to do something about it? It doesn't necessarily mean you have to cut them out of your life entirely, but if you do this will, of course, open up the energetic space to bring new people and relationships in.

Now that we've looked at decluttering from a physical and lifestyle perspective; has it made you realise the extent of what you've been holding onto? And from an emotional perspective, holding onto physical clutter may also highlight the fact you've been used to putting up with a lot of crap in your life. If you have, make a commitment to yourself that this has to stop, NOW! If you don't, you'll be seriously sabotaging your efforts to move on.

OK, so now it's time to tackle the most important part of the entire decluttering process. In order for you to step into your secret power and manifest your dreams, it's essential you clear all your mental and emotional clutter. This includes any limiting beliefs and negative self-talk, excuses, worries, to-do lists, grievances, regrets and resentments. Old memories, past hurts, negative experiences and resentments can massively affect your enjoyment of life and most definitely hold you back. If you've already taken on board some of the tools and techniques from previous chapters,

this part should be a doddle! But let's take a look at some
more practical steps:

- If you've got a never-ending to-do list in your head,
  then writing it down can help to free up mental
  space. Or you may prefer to use an online tool or
  App. Once you have your list, always prioritise and
  tackle the most important tasks first, and if you
  don't get through it by the end of the day, don't
  keep carrying tasks forward. There is nothing more
  demoralising; plus your mindset will be all wrong.
  Ask yourself why you've not got everything
  finished. Have you been procrastinating because
  you're fearful of the task? Or has life got in the
  way? Don't make excuses, but at the same time, it's
  important you're honest with yourself as it could be
  due to setting unrealistic expectations. You could
  try limiting the number of tasks you add to your to-
  do list each day, to a maximum of five, for example.
  Something else you might like to try that I have
  found useful is to write a 'to-done' list at the end of
  the day, which focuses on what you have achieved
  (however small and insignificant it may seem),
  rather than that frustrating to-do list. It's a much
  more positive approach, and what you achieve may
  pleasantly surprise you.
- Since mind clutter is often related to things that
  have occurred in the past, letting go is an essential

element of decluttering, and as resentment is a
biggie, forgiveness is key. (You may like to re-read
the chapter on forgiveness to help with this.) What I
encourage you to do is create a list and note down
every single thing you can remember, from your
earliest memories in childhood to the present day,
of any event, experience or person you've so far
been unable to forgive. Don't forget; this may
include yourself. It could be an occasion you
remember from when you were very young, and
your mum shouted at you for something that
wasn't your fault or a particular event at school
where someone was really mean to you. It could be
an embarrassing memory from work or a time you
lent money to a friend and they didn't pay it back.
Or it could be something you perceive to have
failed at or wished you'd handled differently. Write
EVERYTHING down on your list, until you're
satisfied it's complete and then comes the important
part. Now you must go back over your list, tackling
every person, situation or experience one by one
and FORGIVE. Acknowledge that by doing this you
are freeing yourself of emotional baggage that will
otherwise keep rearing its ugly head and continue
to hold you back. Yes, this will be a time-consuming
task, but skip it at your peril! Simply spend some
time going down the list (and it doesn't have to be
completed in one go), briefly think about the person

or experience and say something along the lines of; sorry, please forgive me, thank you. And if you attach an 'I love you' at the end, this will be especially powerful.

- Don't forget the other tools at your disposal, like affirmations and EFT. They are both powerful techniques to address and release negative thought patterns or self-limiting beliefs, while the benefits of meditation to clear mental clutter are profound. And remember, if you really struggle with the forgiveness part, call upon your angels and the Universe to help you.

AWARE: I hope this chapter has made you aware of the enormous impact clutter can have on your life. A messy room, cupboard, car or office space has far greater implications on your health, mental wellbeing and life goals, than merely the distraction of the clutter itself. Really use this to your advantage. With awareness comes power and the opportunity to do something about it.

ADJUST: Gradually work your way through the tips and recommendations I have given you to declutter every aspect of your life. It's likely you'll think of more things as you go along and if so, go with it. I can't stress enough the importance of decluttering properly. Failure to do so will result in things coming back to bite you, so don't gloss over this section! It will get easier, as with the more space you free up, the better and more motivated you'll feel to keep at it. Make all the adjustments necessary, and you'll be so grateful you did.

ATTRACT: The very process of decluttering creates an energetic space to attract new things and allow them to flow into your life. Whether you're thinking about long-term goals or dreams at the moment, for peace of mind and a stress-free life, you owe it to yourself to clear out the trash!

ALLOWING - GOAL SETTING

The first step to manifesting abundance is to recognise and really appreciate what you already have, as this will instantly raise your vibration and put you in a much better position to allow and receive. But it also helps to set goals, and now that you've decluttered your life and created that solid foundation, you're good to go! Even so, if you're new to goal setting, it may seem a bit daunting and perhaps unnecessary, but I really encourage you to do it. And the best place to start is to determine what it is you really desire. Sounds simple enough, right? Yet many of us struggle at this first hurdle.

The first time I was asked as an adult to give serious thought to my goals and dreams was when I joined a network marketing company. I remember actually cringing at the time and was genuinely at a complete loss as to what to say. What was I supposed to say? I'd had dreams as a kid, and they'd always seemed to be wrong in some way. I frantically delved into the inner recesses of my brain, desperate to come up with some tangible goals, but I was terrified of being laughed at or judged. It was almost like I'd suddenly found myself standing there naked and I was very uncomfortable.

I was prompted for my answer and genuinely thought I was going to have a panic attack. It's not like it was a formal meeting or anything, but a cup of coffee with a friend, so why did the whole experience make me feel so uncomfortable? And I certainly wasn't unique here. Countless times as I went on to ask the same question of others, during my years in the business, I found so many reacted in a very similar way. Not only are we not encouraged to set goals and so the entire process is very alien to us, but if and when we are, we tend to fit them around the constraints of our current lifestyle, rather than allowing ourselves to open up to the possibilities and dream.

I think a lot of it has to do with expectations and not wanting to be judged. When we're put on the spot like I was, it's all too easy to worry and overthink, searching for the right answer when there simply isn't one. Your goals and dreams are very personal to you, and the last thing that should concern you is what anyone else thinks. Not only that but they will change over time. As you achieve some of your goals, you'll almost certainly have others to take their place. At least I'd encourage this, as it's how you grow.

"Whatever the mind can conceive and believe, it can achieve…"

— NAPOLEON HILL

See if you can relate to these three typical stumbling blocks to goal setting:

1. You don't know what you really want. Based on what society tells you or what your friends, family or neighbours have, you've decided it'd be nice to have more money or live in a bigger house, to get a promotion at work or have your own business, to lose weight, or to get married and start a family. But are they really your goals and dreams? As I've said, we're so rarely asked as adults to set personal goals that we don't really give them serious thought, or even know where to start. We fall into the trap of basing our goals around what we think they 'should' be, or what others want or expect for us. Some people even forget how to dream, or are scared to because they don't believe they'll come true, especially if they've been knocked back time after time in the past. No wonder we have such difficulty setting them! As children, we are asked all the time what we want to be when we grow up, and we have no problem thinking big. We have no concept of perception, or whether or not our dreams

are entirely realistic. We don't overcomplicate, over analyse or ask anyone's permission, we just dream. If we want to be the queen of England or fly to the moon, then this is what we'll set our hearts on. Until someone tells us not to be ridiculous, of course, or that we're not smart enough, or it's impossible. And this is how we learn to shrink our dreams or worse, give up on them completely, in order to conform to a life our friends, family or society tells us is right for us. But how many things are we grateful for now that were once deemed impossible, like flying? How many people in history were ridiculed for their inventive ideas, or told it simply couldn't be achieved? Fortunately for us, they didn't give up on their dreams.

2. You know what you want and have tried goal-setting before, but without success. This could be due to not having completed the all-important decluttering work first, or because you didn't go about the actual goal-setting process properly. You may have set your sights too small or at completely the other end of the scale and way too high. If you don't attempt to expand your thinking, believe anything is possible and dream big, then you may lack enthusiasm for your goals and not really 'feel' them. But equally, if your dreams are way too big and scary, and you really don't believe there's a hope in hell of ever achieving them, or understand

the importance of breaking them down, then you'll risk setting yourself up for failure right from the get-go.

3. You know your goals, but have a real FEAR of FAILURE, and this is a common one. You're scared to death that if you reveal your goals to someone else and, heaven forbid say them out loud, then you'll be held accountable. What happens if you don't then achieve them? EVERYONE will know you failed! In which case you may well conclude that it's safer not to set goals at all…

Of course, this is rubbish. I challenge you to research any highly successful person and not see a whole string of 'failures' behind them. I can almost guarantee this is what you'll find, yet it's all too easy to think otherwise. You imagine they've not had to deal with the challenges you have, or that they have more influential contacts, or it's all down to luck or money. But it doesn't matter whether it's an Olympic athlete, a rock star, or an entrepreneur business tycoon like Sir Richard Branson, they will have all suffered setbacks and failures to get to where they are now. Not just that, but we don't see what goes on in the background. Think of all the years and years of training for the athlete before we see them at their peak, or of how many rock stars rise up after a personal battle with drugs or alcohol. And as for Sir Richard Branson, you only have to read one of his books to see how many of his business ventures failed, some quite spectacularly, before he reached the height of his success.

So how come they're successful? Of course, it's partly due to the fact they're driven, motivated and passionately connected to their goals which is a key factor, but it's also very much because they learn from their perceived failures. If they suffer a setback, it doesn't make them give up or shy away from setting new goals; in fact, they're more likely to set even bigger and bolder ones. As I've said, it's all a matter of perception anyway. What one person may view as a failure, another can see as a stepping stone on the road to success.

Definitely don't put off setting goals because of a fear of failure. And if you believe you've already failed at something, then I urge you to view it as a mere bump in the road instead. It may have delayed your route to success, but it will not stop you. There is no such thing as failure anyway; view it as feedback on your journey.

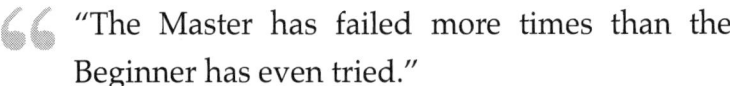 "The Master has failed more times than the Beginner has even tried."

In her book 'The Top Five Regrets of the Dying', palliative nurse Bronnie Ware asked her patients if there was anything they would have done differently and the number one answer was that they wished they'd had the courage to a live a life that was true to themselves and not one that was expected of them. Facing death made them realise how many of their dreams had gone unfulfilled. There was no mention of things they'd failed at, but regrets of playing small, making do in life rather than taking more risks and stepping outside of their comfort zones, and for not taking their happiness more seriously.

Having said all of this, do bear in mind of course that if things really don't go to plan or you find yourself up against way too much resistance, it may be a gentle nudge from your angels and the Universe that you'd be better off doing some tweaking, or following a different path!

The Goal Setting Process

- Set Clear Goals - Really take time to get clear about what YOU want. Make your goals personal and don't worry about what others might think, say or expect of you. Remember they don't need to resemble any of the stereotypical goals I mentioned earlier. It could be that you want to go vegan, give up smoking, or commit to meditating every day. You may then decide to keep your goal to yourself, or tell others because you want support, or to be held accountable, but don't let anyone put you off or tell you it can't be done!
- Connect - Make sure you really connect with your goals. Ideally, they should either light you up inside or scare you, but in an excited kind of way. Think of

a child with the anticipation of Christmas. Ask yourself important questions around your goals to help you with this, like how it would make you feel if you achieved them? How would it change your life? What would be different? If you did opt for a more money goal, then why? What would you be spending it on? Really 'feel' into your goal setting. The more you're able to connect with them, the better equipped you'll be to face those bumps in the road.

- Ask - Don't forget to ask your angels and the Universe to help guide you if you're still unsure. Don't just set goals for the sake of it.
- Write Them Down - You may have heard of the saying a dream written down with a date becomes a goal. Whatever your goals are, studies have consistently shown that the simple act of writing them down can make a huge difference to the outcome. Even the prestigious Harvard University has studied this and how it can help bridge the gap between simply having goals and, more importantly, achieving them. The idea of then adding dates to them is to fuel your motivation, as well as give you something tangible to work towards. As the great Napolean Hill said, "A goal is a dream with a deadline". So, what are you waiting for? Grab a pen and get started!
- Break Them Down - Just a word of warning before

you get too carried away though. While you need to consider your big picture goals (that big dream that might scare you), it is then essential you break it down into smaller, more manageable, bite-size pieces. There are a couple of reasons for this. On the one hand, you don't want to become too overwhelmed with your goal that it puts you off before you start, but also by achieving smaller wins along the way it'll help you build your confidence and self-belief as you move towards the bigger goals. Let me give you an example here, and a really clear one is with my karate.

I had just turned forty years old when I started full contact, knockdown karate. Now in the first instance, this was met with a very mixed response, not least that I was having a midlife crisis! It could very easily have put me off going. But I really wanted to do it for me. In fact, I'd secretly wanted to for years, but had never had the confidence, so when an opportunity presented itself, I was straight on it. Now I'm not going to pretend it was easy; in fact, I found it extremely daunting as a woman of that age to take her first class. Fortunately, I was met with an amazing group of people who very quickly became my karate family. But let me get back to goal setting…

To be honest, I never set my sights on becoming a black belt, not at first anyway. This really did seem like an impossible dream. I remember my first real goal was to achieve my blue belt, and even this was three gradings down the line. But I had a definite plan, and my goal was clearly broken down. I knew that to achieve my blue belt I first had to pass two red belt gradings. The gradings at that level were three months apart, and I had to complete a set number of classes before I could attend the grading. I had a grading sheet, and each class was ticked off as I attended and so I knew without any shadow of a doubt whether or not I was on track. Obviously, I had to train hard and learn the syllabus, but all the steps were clearly defined. And I could celebrate each milestone success as I went along.

I was as thrilled to pass my very first grading as I was months later when I finally achieved my blue belt. I also knew by then that I wanted to take it further, which is exactly why I've said you should review your goals from time to time as they will change. I was still not ready to believe I could become an actual black belt one day, but I took it one step at a time and gradually worked my way up the grades.

Of course, by doing this, that goal of becoming a black belt started to get more realistic. I knew it wouldn't be easy and would test my body, mind and soul to the max, but it was becoming believable to me. And so, five years after having taken my very first class and literally through blood, sweat and tears, I completed a six-hour grading to achieve my black belt. It still remains one of my greatest personal achievements ever.

Not only that but I went on to teach karate for a year, a class of adults and children, and ended up taking my second dan two years later. All of this was achieved because I set a clear goal that was very personal to me (that I reviewed over time), and I wouldn't let any negativity put me off from achieving it. Plus I broke it down into doable steps. I was also prepared to leave my comfort zone and do what was necessary to achieve it, which brings me onto my final steps.

- Celebrate Your Wins - This is so important. It doesn't matter how small it may seem to you; you must make a point of noticing what you've achieved. As I've already mentioned, this will go a long way to build your confidence and make that seemingly impossible goal appear more within reach. The celebration can be whatever you want it to be. It can be to treat yourself to a massage or read a good book, or to meet up with friends for lunch. It doesn't matter, just so long as you recognise your win in some way.
- ACTION - Goal setting is important, as is the law of attraction and ensuring your vibration is a match to what you desire, but no amount of either will result in success unless you also take some action towards them. The Universe wants to see you are serious! I couldn't just dream about becoming a black belt and not put in the work, any more than someone

who wants to run a marathon or win an Olympic gold medal can if they don't put in the necessary training. Your action steps don't need to be huge, but any small and consistent step towards your goal is a step in the right direction. A lot of this part is down to mindset. Sadly, some people are so fearful of leaving their comfort zone to take the action steps required that they never even get started. But what I've found time and time again is that the stress of taking action is usually far worse than just getting on and doing it. Can you relate to times in your life where you've noticed this? I bet you can!

- Plan; Do; Review - This step is important. Be prepared that your goals will change and so you need to regularly review them. You may even need to change direction slightly. Remember that when you release your desires to the Universe and really let go of the outcome, it may have better ideas for you! Be open to the possibilities.

If after all this, you're still struggling with knowing how you want your future to look and with the whole process of goal setting, then it may be helpful for you to consider these questions:

- If money was no object and you had no fear whatsoever over anyone's opinion, or of being judged, what would you want to be, do or have?

- If there was absolutely no possibility of failure, what would you want to do?
- What really, really matters to you?
- WHO really matters to you? I mean in the grand scheme of things if everything did go pear-shaped, who would you be most upset about letting down? I bet it wouldn't be as many people as you think. I mean honestly, if your neighbour ended up thinking you were a failure, is it really worth losing sleep over? Of course not.

And so finally, don't overcomplicate the process or worry about what others think and just go for it!

AWARE: Are you clear about the goal-setting process now? Are you aware of what you really, really want? Are you 100% sure they are your dreams and not someone else's? Do you have a strong emotional connection to them? Remember that it's this connection that will help you stay motivated if the going gets tough.

ADJUST: What adjustments can you make to ensure success on your goal setting journey? Are you ready to commit to getting that plan down on paper and breaking your journey down into doable steps? Are you ready to take INSPIRED ACTION?

ATTRACT: The whole process of goal setting is simply an effective way to create a structured plan, to help you achieve your dreams, and keep you focused and on track. If you're serious about creating a better future, isn't it worth your best shot? Wouldn't it be better to know that you tried and 'failed', rather than live a life of fear and regret? You don't help anyone by playing small, least of all yourself. You owe it to the world to shine your light! Why do we try so hard to fit in and conform to other people's versions of how our life should be when we can stand out and really make a difference? Yes, it can be scary, and yes, it's a sad fact that not everyone likes seeing others succeed, or simply growing as a person, so be prepared, you may lose some friendships along the way. But I can almost guarantee you'll attract others who are much more on your wavelength and will be more than happy to carry the torch with you. Your vibe attracts your tribe! And anyway, there's no such thing as failure is there?

CREATING A LASER-LIKE FOCUS

Now that we've looked at goal setting, I'd like to bring in a couple of additional techniques that can really help with the allowing and manifestation process. You must create a laser-like focus towards what you want to attract into your life, whether it's better health, money, a new relationship, career or whatever. With clarity and focus comes intention, and this is where the real power lies. So do you now know how you want your future to look and who you want to become?

DREAM BOARDS

A great, visual way of connecting with your goals is to create a dream board, also known as a vision or goal board. You may have come across this concept before as they're regularly used as part of the law of attraction process, as well as when setting personal development or business goals. To explain in very basic terms, you just pin pictures that correspond to your goals, dreams and desires, onto a simple notice board. If you want to manifest a new car for example, then you'd find a picture corresponding to the exact make, model and colour of the car and add it to your dream board. If you dream of doing yoga on the beach, then you'd find a picture depicting this and add it to your board etc. Some people also like to add quotes and personal affirmations.

But much more than just randomly sticking a few pictures or quotes on a cork-board, it's about making them personal and special to you, just as with your goal setting. You should take time to connect with your higher self during the process. Some people like to make quite a ritual over creating their dream board and may meditate beforehand to gain clarity of thought, light a candle and play some beautiful, inspirational music, and then set their intention. None of this is necessary, but it does help signify its importance to you (and the Universe), so makes for a powerful intention.

Of course, if you've already taken time to consider your goals and I very much hope that you have by now, then creating your dream board should be relatively easy. You want to be able to look at it and see exactly how you want your future to unfold, and so the more detailed, the better. If for example one of your desires is to have your own home, then will it be a cottage in the countryside, an apartment in the city, or a glass-fronted house by the ocean? Will you have a garden full of flowers and a peaceful spot where you can meditate? How many bedrooms will it have? Will it be modern and contemporary in style, or traditional or quaint? Find pictures to illustrate all of this. Really let your imagination run wild and have fun with it.

Once your dream board is finished, it's important to hang it in a place you'll notice it frequently, as the idea behind it is to keep reinforcing into your subconscious mind your very specific desires. Remember we learn through repetition, and your subconscious can't distinguish between what is real and what is not, so the more often you look at the pictures, the better. And when you look at them, allow yourself to feel really excited and as though you've already achieved them. Not only will this help to raise your vibration and put you in a better frequency to attract what you want, but it'll also help distract you from negative thoughts, doubts and that pain in the ass critical self-talk. Your vision board acts as a constant, positive reminder of how you want your future to look and it'll help to spur you on when things aren't going quite to plan and remind you of WHY you are doing what you're doing. So what are you waiting for?

VISUALISATION

Another powerful technique that you will have already done whether consciously or not is visualisation. When I've asked you to get really clear about your goals, and when you were choosing the pictures for your dream board you will have been visualising how you want your future to look and your future self to be. It's just like painting pictures in your mind. Some people find this really easy and can conjure up really bright, colourful and detailed images, while for others it can take a bit of time and practice. But don't think you can't do it.

If I was to ask you right now NOT to imagine a bright yellow butterfly, what's the very first thing that would come into your mind? Or to give you another example, how about when you read a novel and can follow the story? You will have been creating images in your mind. I very much doubt the book would have contained actual pictures, yet you are able to imagine the characters and scenes within the story, based on how the author describes them. The same is true with visualising your goals and dreams; only now, you are the author and the artist. You are imagining and creating your own story.

Think back to the example I gave about the new home and how I asked you to imagine it in detail. You should be able to see it in your mind's eye, walk through the front door and around the entire building — the more detailed and specific the picture is in your mind, the better. And you'll know when you're creating a vision to match your desire, as you'll feel excited, happy, proud even if you are visualising an achievement. You'll almost certainly become aware that you're smiling like a Cheshire cat, or have butterflies inside.

Some people find it easier to imagine they are in a movie theatre, watching their lives unfold on the big screen before them. Since they are the hero in the story, they can basically create whatever they want. Once again, the detail is important, as is using as many of our senses as possible. So we imagine not only what we see, but any sounds that may be around us and also what we can smell, feel and potentially even taste too. And then to ramp up the power of this visualisation even more, we can even imagine entering the actual screen, becoming part of the movie itself and so looking out through our own eyes.

Writing down an entire script around your visualisation can be another powerful tool. Or a letter to yourself, or a page in a diary dated sometime in the future where you outline your perfect day and what it looks like to you. The possibilities are endless!

However you choose to do your visualisation practice, I would encourage you to make it a part of your daily routine. It doesn't need to be complicated or take hours of your time, in fact, it need only be for a few minutes at first, but consistency and practice are important. A perfect time to visualise your dreams is when you go to bed at night, as they'll be the last thing on your mind before you drift off to sleep and this will really help lock them into your subconscious mind. Just allow yourself to get comfortable and into a relaxed state, focus on your breathing, and then dream in glorious technicolour! Remember you are looking to create those strong, intense connections, emotions and feelings.

Once you start visualising regularly, you'll very quickly become aware of the endless possibilities. Not just reserved for major life goals and dreams, but to help with positive outcomes for exams, interviews, public speaking, surgery, you name it. I have used it when I've been on courses and then imagined my name on the pass certificate, when taking my karate gradings and all the time when my husband was sick, visualising his cancer-free body.

Interestingly as I studied mindset in the run-up to my black belt grading, I came across studies where athletes had used visualisation to great effect. Such is the power of visualisation that when Russian athletes used this technique for the 1976 Olympic games and won more gold medals than any other country, they were actually accused of cheating! But long before then, back in 1954, Roger Bannister relentlessly visualised his success in breaking the four-minute barrier to run a mile. This was believed to be physically impossible... until he proved everyone wrong!

And within the sporting arena, other impressive studies have since been carried out. There are numerous studies where athletes are assigned to different groups to either continue their training as normal without using visualisation or by using it to some degree to imagine they are training, with the results being quite astounding. In fact, those who had actively participated in their sport only 25% of the time but who had visualised themselves training the remaining 75%, outperformed those who simply trained, or had trained to a greater degree than visualised. How impressive is that? Such is the power of the mind. Since mental imagery has become more recognised as a way to condition the brain for successful outcomes, it has been implemented by many top performers. The proof is there. The more we mentally rehearse something in our mind, the more it habitually becomes.

In order to prepare for my black belt grading, I used visualisation in several different ways. I imagined myself perfecting my karate techniques and katas, and getting through the exercises and fights. I knew I'd be required to do a hundred push-ups and they'd never been my strong point, so I visualised myself doing them just as much as I physically trained for them. And I knew I'd be called out to teach the entire group at some point, which totally freaked me out. I was terrified my mind would go blank with nerves, and so I imagined this going really well, of being relaxed, confident and able to teach accurately. And, of course, I visualised myself in the crowded sports hall at the end of the grading, being congratulated and handed my black belt, bursting with pride. I knew without a shadow of a doubt how overwhelming this moment would be, in a good way, so that was pretty easy! And I'm delighted to say, it all panned out almost exactly as I'd visualised it - I even managed the push-ups!

It's thanks to your feel-good emotions that you'll raise your vibration and better connect to the frequency of what you want to manifest. Visualisation activates your creative subconscious, and as I've said before, this can't distinguish between what is real and what isn't. As a result, your brain searches for ways to bring you the resources you need to achieve the outcome you want, activating the law of attraction. Furthermore, by visualising your dreams, you'll give your motivation a massive boost, which in turn will help you stay on track to keep going until they manifest.

AWARE: Are you aware now of the immense power of visualisation and how you can use it to bring about the outcomes you want? And can you see how creating your own dream board can help magnify the power of this process?

ADJUST: Can you visualise in detail your goals and dreams? If you've created dream boards before, or visualised without success, are there any adjustments you can make to how you've gone about it? Perhaps you're still not entirely clear about your goals, or are failing to connect with your dreams? Or maybe it just needs updating?

ATTRACT: When you consistently visualise your dreams, as though they've already been achieved, you rapidly accelerate the entire manifestation process. If you're ready to step into your secret power and attract all your heart desires, what are you waiting for?

PART 4 - ACHIEVE SELF-MASTERY & MIRACLES

YOUR SECRET POWER

We've been on such an incredible journey together, and I hope it's given you a much clearer understanding of how limiting beliefs, negative thought patterns and your ego can all play a part in keeping you stuck and preventing you from reaching your highest potential. But I hope I've also given you faith that it doesn't have to be this way. YOU absolutely have the power to break free of these constraints and really step into your secret power. From tidying up your diet to taking advantage of the amazing techniques I've introduced you to, to quieting your mind, connecting with your angels and harnessing the power of pure essential oils, you really have everything you need to raise your vibration and nourish your body, mind and soul. And we finished by looking at the law of attraction and goal setting to put you in the best position to manifest your desires and achieve the life you want. Now it's up to you to take on board what you've learned, decide you're no longer prepared to settle and move forward to achieve self-mastery and miracles.

But before I bid you farewell and wave you off on your adventure, let's just consider some final, key points.

BE AUTHENTIC: Always be totally authentic to yourself. You're not here to people please and live the dreams of others, or to put up with a mediocre existence. You're here to find your true purpose, that calling that really lights you up inside. You don't serve anyone by playing small, but neither will you if you're not being true to yourself. If you constantly worry about what others think of you, or that by speaking up you may upset someone, then this is only going to create unease, fear and frustration for you. It's all well and good trying to be the person you think everyone expects you to be, but it'll prevent you from connecting to your higher self and rob you of your true happiness. Not only will you be doing a disservice to others by not growing into the person you're meant to be, but it'll be exhausting keeping up the pretence of being someone you're not.

The world doesn't need a clone of someone else. You are a unique human being and as such, have your own very unique gifts to share. By allowing yourself to fully embrace your secret power, love and joy will not only flow within you but far outside too. And this will have a very positive influence on those around you.

Speaking your truth and living an authentic life is a massive part of self-mastery and you'll quickly notice just how empowering it is. Take responsibility for your life NOW. You are in the driving seat, and only you can create the change necessary to move you towards living your best life. Even if you're still feeling nervous about your onward journey and are struggling to quieten your critical self-talk, remember that simply by being aware of it, you are making progress. With awareness comes choice. You can either continue to think and act as you always have and not expect a different outcome, or you can use this awareness to your advantage and make a decision to start creating new beliefs.

SHARE YOUR VULNERABILITY: Part of being authentic is to not be scared to reveal your vulnerability. This can be a difficult one, on the one hand, because you may not want to 'own up' to when life sucks and isn't going to plan, but also you may fear it as a sign of weakness (as I did), or of burdening someone else with your problems. But this couldn't be further from the truth. As I've mentioned before, being brave enough to share your vulnerability is a strength, something I've learned over the years, and you'll find that the genuine people in your life will respect you for it and want to help if they can. Plus you'll be able to help others in the long run.

When my husband got so desperately ill, I was reluctant at first to share how I was struggling to cope. Not only because I'd fallen right back into believing it was a weakness on my part, but also due to the feelings of guilt that if I was supported it'd take the emphasis off him and his healing. But when I did open up, not only did it allow others to show an overwhelming amount of love and support to us as a family, but it also meant I was able to pay this kindness forwards. The knowledge of what we were going through prompted a couple of friends to get in touch and reveal they were in a similar situation, and this, in turn, enabled me to support them. If I hadn't shared what I was going through, this wouldn't have been possible.

Another example is seeking perfection. When I first started doing Facebook live videos for my business, I nearly drove myself mad trying to make them as perfect as I possibly could. I'd have a meltdown if my dog barked or the phone rang in the middle of what I was doing and when I watched my video back after I'd finished I'd always find fault. But then it occurred to me. No one wants perfect. Of course, this doesn't mean people are waiting and hoping to see you stuff up! It just makes you normal. And think about how much more relatable you'll be as a person if those around you see your setbacks as well as your triumphs? If you're doing your utmost to portray a perfect, happy and successful lifestyle, if the complete opposite is true, you won't win many supporters. In fact, most people will see through it a mile off, and you'll end up losing your credibility.

BE KIND: Always be kind to yourself and to others. Genuine acts of kindness will raise your vibration and make you feel amazing. And if you're experiencing an off day, or feel you've slipped back into victim mentality, it's a really effective way to shift your focus away from your own problems. Your angels and the Universe will be only too pleased to support you, as sincere acts of kindness are steeped in love.

BE FORGIVING: Part of being kind is to be forgiving. Don't forget that by holding onto past resentments or regrets, you are only hurting yourself, and sabotaging your own personal and spiritual growth. No person, situation or experience is worth this sacrifice.

BE PRESENT: Remember to live in the NOW. Make the most of every moment of every day and factor in as much quality time as you can with the people you love and who mean the most to you. Don't waste precious moments living in the past and clinging onto old regrets or hurts, but equally don't miss out on your journey by always looking too far ahead.

BE AWARE: Now you understand the importance of raising your awareness, use it to your advantage by stopping negative thought patterns and limiting beliefs in their tracks. Tap to release, use affirmations, or simply try the 'cancel, clear, delete'. Just don't beat yourself up or get into judgement mode. Obviously, you'll also need to be aware of negative people or situations, so aim to spend the majority of your time with people who raise your vibration and not with the mood hoovers! But do bear in mind that if you're vibrating at a lower level yourself, you'll attract people of the same frequency, just as when you start raising your vibe these same people may naturally fall away and out of your life.

BE HOLISTIC: Be mindful of adopting a holistic approach to nurture your body, mind and soul. Base your diet around fresh, nourishing, high vibe foods, spend time outside in nature and with animals, and take some time out for personal reflection and meditation every day. I'd also encourage you to move and stretch your body on a daily basis too, by adding in some form of regular exercise. A walk outside in the fresh air is a perfect example although, ideally, you'll want to include an activity to increase your heart rate alongside some strength training too. Now, this doesn't mean you have to join a gym and pump iron if this isn't for you. Bodyweight exercises like push-ups are great for strength training, as are Pilates and Yoga.

The biggest tip I can give you with regards to exercise is to find something you enjoy doing, as you'll be far more likely to keep it up. It doesn't matter if it's walking, jogging, dancing, cycling, horse riding or karate. It's also a great idea to enlist the support of a friend and work out together, as this will help to hold you accountable, increase motivation and make it more fun too! Your body loves to move, and the benefits of exercise are undisputed.

Nourish your body, mind and soul, and you'll be nurturing your life force energy and raising your vibration. Not only will you feel amazing, but you'll be unstoppable too!

PLAY TO YOUR STRENGTHS: Another good tip is to play to your strengths. If you know you're particularly good at something, or have an especially strong characteristic or attribute, then use it to your advantage. If you struggle to think of anything, it may be easier for you to consider what your friends, family or co-workers often praise you for. Perhaps it's that you're an excellent communicator or have great leadership qualities? Or that you're honest and kind? And if you're really stuck, or are interested in delving into this a little deeper, you can even take a free online survey to work out your strengths, via an organisation like the VIA Institute. I've included their link in the resource section of the book.

SURRENDER: Let go of the need to receive and focus instead on what you can give. This doesn't mean going to the other extreme and not allowing yourself to receive, but shifting your focus, surrendering to the Universe and letting go of the outcome. If you are always looking to see what you can get out of doing something, your energy will be wrong, and any reward may evade you.

Shifting your focus will also be extremely useful at those times you'll need to step outside of your comfort zone. Say, for example, it's been a dream of yours to work with a particular person, but you've never had the courage to approach them about it. You're so worried what they'll think, or if they'll turn you down, that you just end up stressing over all the possible outcomes. But it may be because you're focusing on what YOU have to gain. Say instead you redirect your focus onto the other person, and potentially all the benefits they'd gain if you worked together? Now, don't you see how the energy shifts, making it easier for you to approach them? It's almost like you owe it to them. Instead of worrying about YOU, you can see how you'll be doing this other person a disservice if you don't discuss your proposal.

Another example. Perhaps you've been asked to talk to a group of people about a challenge you've overcome, and the thought of it scares you to death. If you focus on yourself, your emotions and potentially everything that could go wrong, you may end up making excuses and not doing it. But if you shift your focus onto all the people you may be able to help, to give them hope there is light at the end of the tunnel, do you not see how much easier it will be to stand up there and give the talk? Especially when you know what they're going through.

And of course, I've also discussed with you the importance of surrendering your goals and dreams to the Universe too. Even when you know exactly what you want and have set your intention, it's vital you let go of the outcome as things may not work out in the way you expect them to. The Universe may have other plans for you, to bring you something even better! Keep an open mind and trust that all will be revealed in perfect divine timing. You are exactly where you're meant to be right now.

YOUR DAILY ROUTINE

With all the tools and techniques I've presented to you, it goes without saying that they'll only work if you actually use them. Consistently. I'm sure you'd have no problem understanding the need to exercise regularly if you want a toned and fit body. You'd not be able to achieve a six-pack if you only ever performed a couple of crunches here and there. Well, the same is true for your personal and spiritual growth. Change takes time; particularly lasting change, which is what you're after. Plus this is a lifelong journey remember!

Creating a daily routine will increase your chances of success, and it takes about 21 days to form a new habit. Once your daily routine becomes a habit, just like cleaning your teeth, you'll find it second nature to stick to. And once you start to notice the benefits of your new routine, how much calmer and more focused you are, while at the same time being more empowered and motivated, you'll want to keep at it. You'll also be hungry to learn more.

How you begin each day really sets the tone for how it will unfold in its entirety. I'm sure you'll have experienced those days when everything seems to go wrong, and you catch yourself thinking (or being told) that you got out of bed the wrong side? If your day begins in a negative way, it's typical to descend on a downward spiral throughout the rest of it. But start your day in a positive way, and transformation and miracles are yours for the taking!

Before we run through an example of a positive routine, let's just take a moment to set some ground rules... If you're serious about starting your day in the best possible way, this does NOT include checking your phone, social media, emails or 'to-do' lists! In fact, I STRONGLY recommend you don't even take your mobile phone to your bedroom at night. I can't stress this enough. You want to start your day with a clear head and a positive mindset, and you'll achieve neither if you pick up that phone!

Your Morning Routine

- INTENTION: As soon as you wake every morning, set an intention for the day. Something positive, obviously! A simple but powerful example could be that this will be your best day ever and that you're open to all the great experiences and abundance coming your way.
- HYDRATE: Drink a glass of water on rising, ideally with the juice of half a lemon squeezed into it. Not only will this help to hydrate your body, but it's also very cleansing for your liver.
- MEDITATE: Set aside some time to meditate in a

quiet space. You'll want to be warm and comfortable, but not so comfortable you fall back to sleep. Set an intention before you meditate, as this really offers it up to the Universe. And remember you can ask for answers to any questions you may have to be revealed to you during your meditation or just ask to be guided. I like to say thank you for revealing to me what I need to know. Aim for 20 minutes of meditation, but build this up gradually if need be.

- GRATITUDE: Write down at least three to five things you're grateful for and remember you can include gratitude for things yet to come. If you have more time, you may like to write your thoughts, affirmations and what you're grateful for in more detail in a journal.

- VISUALISE: Spend a few moments visualising how you'd like your day to unfold, or thinking about your future goals.

- READ / LISTEN: Another great practice if you have time, is to read a few pages of a positive or inspirational book, or listen to a podcast along the same lines. Sometimes I'll listen to a podcast as I'm walking my dog in the morning.

- EXERCISE: Even if it's just a few stretches - your body will thank you for it.

OK, so now that you have your list are you already thinking there's no way you'd have the time to do it all? Haha, I thought you might! But believe it or not, there's nothing on there that needs to take a vast amount of time. Five minutes meditating is better than none and if you seriously don't have time to write down all that you're grateful for, then just offer up your thanks before you get out of bed, alongside setting your intention for the day.

But the bottom line is this. If you're serious about stepping into your secret power, you will find the time. You may have to get up a little earlier, but it absolutely can be done. So why then leave it here? Why not adopt a great evening routine too?

Evening Routine:

- GRATITUDE: Once again take some time to really think about all the things you're grateful for. It may, of course, be relative to what happened during your day, but it doesn't need to be. Just give thanks for all the abundance in your life.
- JOURNAL: If you like to journal then take a few moments to write down your thoughts. If your day didn't quite go to plan, then rewrite the script! Write down a more positive version of events. Why not?
- VISUALISATION: Often I leave my visualisation until the evening, as I prefer to think about my

goals and dreams as I'm drifting off to sleep. I believe this is a powerful way to really anchor them into your subconscious and plant those seeds. Find what works best for you.

- RELAX: A warm relaxing bath with some magnesium salts added and a few drops of lavender essential oil is a great way to unwind. You may like to read, listen to some music, light some candles and meditate again. Whatever helps you prepare for that all-important time, sleep. Restful sleep is vital for your physical body, mind and soul, so don't neglect it.
- AVOID DRAMA & BLUE LIGHT: What I strongly advise against is watching the news, or even nasty, violent films just before bed. The last thing you need is to be thinking about a lot of negativity as you drift off to sleep - presuming you're even able to sleep! Also avoid working too late into the evening and particularly on your computer or mobile phone, as the blue light it emits is too stimulating for your brain which again means you'll find it more difficult to switch off.

Alongside your daily routine, it's important to factor in some time for doing more of the things you love. What really makes you smile and feel fantastic? Make an intention to treat yourself to some of this 'you time' during your week. Block out time on your calendar for a massage, or to have lunch with a friend, or to finally go on that long, country walk you've promised yourself. Whatever it is, big or small, make time for the moments and experiences that make you feel great. This will be time well spent; it'll do wonders for your vibration! And obviously, you can add in any of the other practices and techniques I've mentioned, just as often as you like.

Self-mastery is a gradual and ongoing process, but I can assure you that by working on every aspect of yourself, you'll see how much stronger you'll become with each passing day. It won't make you immune from having to face challenges, but you'll become more resilient and bounce back quicker. Even for those most painful of experiences in life, the ones that seem to test you to the absolute max, there will come a time when you'll be able to look back and appreciate the space they created for your greatest leaps forward.

So on that note, it's time to end our journey together. Remember to celebrate all your wins, successes, or even the smallest step forward, as they'll help build your confidence and spur you onwards. I actually encourage you to keep track of them by writing them down. This way if you're having a bad day or think that everything seems to be going wrong, you can take a look back and read through your accomplishments. I can almost guarantee it'll put a smile on your face, completely change your mood and raise your vibration! But if it doesn't, then think about a time you felt ecstatically happy, or confident and I'm sure this will do the trick. Just don't beat yourself up if you really are having an off day. It will pass. Take a deep breath and surrender.

I wish you all the very best on your onward journey. You have absolutely got this! Let go of the old and say HELLO to the new you. It's time for you to step into your secret power. It's time for self-mastery, transformation and miracles!

Namaste.

RESOURCES

Below I've included a list of the books I've mentioned, that have been influential to me on my journey, along with other resources I hope you'll find useful. However, just as I continue to grow and evolve, so does my list of recommendations! With that said, if you'd like to keep up-to-date and not miss any of my future suggestions, please head over to www.yoursecretpower.co.uk and sign up for my newsletter, and I'll be able to keep you informed. Thank you.

You Can Heal Your Life; Louise Hay

The Celestine Prophecy; James Redfield

A Course in Miracles; Foundation For Inner Peace

Everything is Here to Help You; Matt Khan

Eat Right 4 Your Type; Dr Peter D'Adamo

The Paleo Diet; Loren Cordain

Fat for Fuel; Joseph Mercola

The No-Grain Diet; Dr Joseph Mercola

Dying To Be Me; Anita Moorjani

Life Changing Foods; The Medical Medium, Anthony William

Angel Prayers; Kyle Gray

The Secret; Rhonda Byrne

Ask & It is Given; Esther & Jerry Hicks

The Top Five Regrets of the Dying; Bronnie Ware

EFT:

The Tapping Solution; Nick Ortner

https://www.thetappingsolution.com/

Brad Yates:

https://www.youtube.com/
channel/UCiHZMZejDS4RIxDdBwoie9A

ThetaHealing®

Introducing an Extraordinary Energy Healing Modality; Vianna Stibal https://www.thetahealing.com/

100% Pure Essential Oils:

https://www.myyl.com/debbiesturge/

VIA Institute for character strengths -

https://www.viacharacter.org/

ABOUT THE AUTHOR

Debbie lives in the seaside town of Margate with her husband Paul and dog Harley. She has two grown children and three grandsons she adores. She loves walking and being outside in nature, and is a self-confessed spirit junkie. She is passionate about living life to the full and not taking anything for granted, and believes that true abundance hinges on good health, a positive mindset and great energetic vibration - total harmony of body, mind and spirit, hence covering all aspects in her work.

After graduating as a nutritional therapist in 1999, Debbie practised in London and from various clinics in Kent and has also tutored for the Institute for Optimum Nutrition. However, while working as a nutritionist, she became aware of the limitations of a purely physical approach to wellness and was led along a more holistic path that incorporated the mind, body and soul. She went on to learn Usui

Reiki in 2014 and has since become a Master/Teacher in both Usui and Angelic Reiki.

Alongside being a therapist, Debbie worked in office management for several years where time after time, she proved her worth and leadership qualities, but it came at a cost. After reaching burnout for the third time in succession, she realised she was not living her true purpose and was being guided by the Universe to work through important lessons. This has resulted in many years of personal/spiritual development and ongoing study, as Debbie admits she is still very much a work in progress and constantly evolving. She is always keen to learn new skills and techniques.

Having been drawn to teaching/mentoring roles over the years, Debbie now shares much of what she has learned in her capacity as a certified Spiritual/Transformation Life Coach and Holistic Wellbeing Expert. She gets immense satisfaction supporting others on their healing journey, and is especially passionate about inspiring women to follow their dreams, believe anything is possible with the right mindset and action and encouraging them to step into their power.

In 2019 Debbie contributed to a powerful book collaboration and became co-author of 'When the Goddess Calls, Volume 2', which hit the Amazon bestseller list within a few hours of its release. A collection of powerful stories from women awakening on their spiritual path, she was honoured to feature alongside twelve other amazing and inspirational women.

As part of her own personal development, Debbie took up full contact karate at age 40 and five years later, after a punishing six-hour grading, was awarded her black belt. She went on to teach her own class for a year and achieved her 2nd Dan two years later.

On her dedicated Facebook page 'Debbie Sturge, Inspiring Change', you'll find regular tips on health, nutrition and exercise, mindset and personal/spiritual development. And on her website, she'll update you with her regular blogs and other resources.

Debbie would love to hear from you!

If you've enjoyed the book and your journey with Debbie so far, please don't keep it to yourself! She'd be delighted if you would share your comments and feedback, so please consider heading over to Amazon and submitting a review. Or email her directly with your experiences and successes.

And if you don't want the journey to end... then why not check out her website and follow the link to schedule a free 15-minute discovery call with her (without obligation)? She'll be able to discuss with you whether a bespoke coaching programme may be an option moving forward and will be happy to answer any questions you may have.

https://www.yoursecretpower.co.uk/

debbie@debbiesturge.com

https://www.myyl.com/debbiesturge/

facebook.com/changewithdebbie

Printed in Poland
by Amazon Fulfillment
Poland Sp. z o.o., Wrocław

61787827R00120